DK CHILDREN'S
ILLUSTRATED REFERENCE
ATLAS

Brian Delf

A Dorling Kindersley Book

DK

LONDON, NEW YORK, MUNICH,
MELBOURNE, DELHI

Editor Lorrie Mack
Designers Adrienne Hutchinson, Andrew O'Brien
Jacket Design Neal Cobourne
DTP Designer Jill Bunyan
Design Manager Jane Thomas
Managing Editor Andrew Macintyre
Category Publisher Sue Grabham
Production Julian Deeming

The material in this book originally appeared in the
Picture Atlas of the World, published in 1996

With thanks to the original team:
Lester Cheeseman, Marcus James, Emma Johnson,
Richard Kemp, Keith Lye, Susan Peach, Roger Priddy,
Teresa Solomon, Kate Woodward, Anna Kunst,
Chris Scollen, Richard Czapnik, Struan Reid,
Cynthia Hole and Luciano Corbella

Published in Great Britain in 2002
by Dorling Kindersley Limited,
80 Strand, London WC2R 0RL
A Penguin company

This edition copyright © 2002
Dorling Kindersley, Limited
Picture Atlas of the World copyright © 1991, 1992
Dorling Kindersley, Limited

A CIP catalogue record for this book is available
from the British Library.

ISBN 0 7513 4759 0

Colour reproduction by Bright Arts, Hong Kong
Printed and bound in Hong Kong by Toppan

Picture credits
(r = right, l = left, t = top, c = centre, b = bottom)
Australian Overseas Information Service, London 45tr, 45br;
Charles Bowman 22t, 22b, 35tr, 35br, 46t; Caribbean Tourist Office
27t; The J. Allan Cash Photolibrary 8tl, 8br, 17tl, 46br;
Lester Cheeseman 37tl, 37tr, 37bc; Chinese Tourist Office 23br;
Egyptian Tourist Office 33tr; Chris Fairclough Colour Library 15tr,
15br, 17r; French Railways Ltd 11cr; Italian State Tourist Office
20t; Norwegian Tourist Office 6tr, 7tr; Roger Priddy 8tr, 11tt, 11br,
46t; Spanish National Tourist Office 19tr; The Telegraph Colour
Library 13b; Travel Photo International 15br, 19b.

Every effort has been made to trace the copyright holders
and we apologise in advance for any unintentional omissions.
We would be pleased to insert the appropriate acknowledgment
in any subsequent edition of this book.

See our complete catalogue at
www.dk.com

CONTENTS

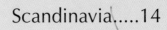

KEY TO THE MAPS

Capital city	**BERLIN** ⊛
City	● **Toronto**
Country name	**J A P A N**
Range of mountains	ALPS
An individual mountain with its height	MT EVEREST 8,848 M
River	Danube
Lake	LAKE COMO
A building or place of special interest	LEANING TOWER OF PISA
A product, animal, plant or activity that is found in the region	*Dairy cattle*

WORLD MAP

ALL THE CONTINENTS except Antarctica are divided into countries, and these vary greatly in size. The largest is the Russian Federation, which stretches across two continents – Europe and Asia. The second largest is Canada, and the third largest is China. In contrast, the smallest country is Vatican City, which lies inside the city of Rome and has an area of only .44 sq km (.17 sq miles). The Russian Federation is almost 39 million times bigger than Vatican City.

LATITUDE AND LONGITUDE

Geographers draw imaginary lines around the globe to help locate places. Lines of latitude run east/west and are measured in degrees from the Equator. Lines of longitude run north/south and are measured in degrees from the Prime Meridian.

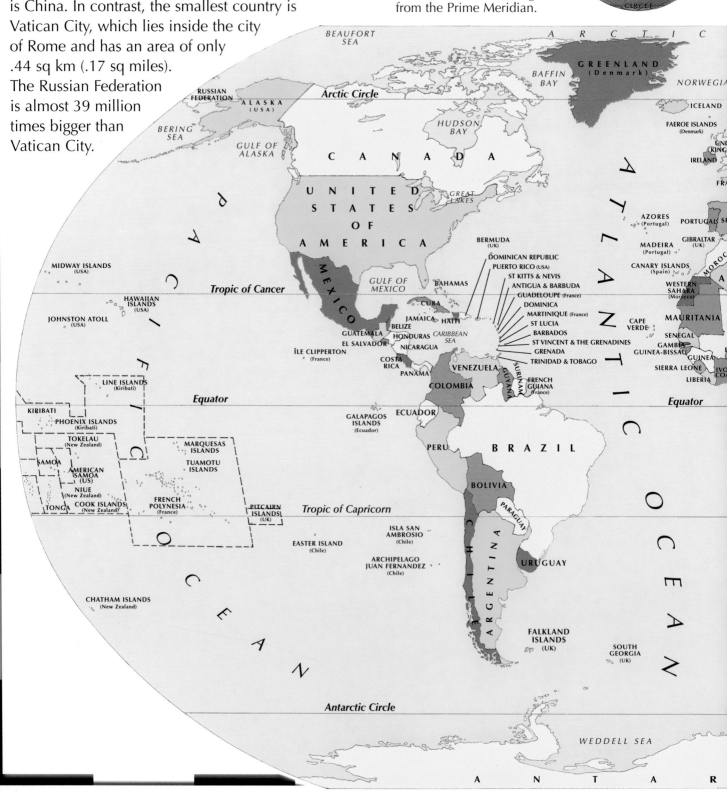

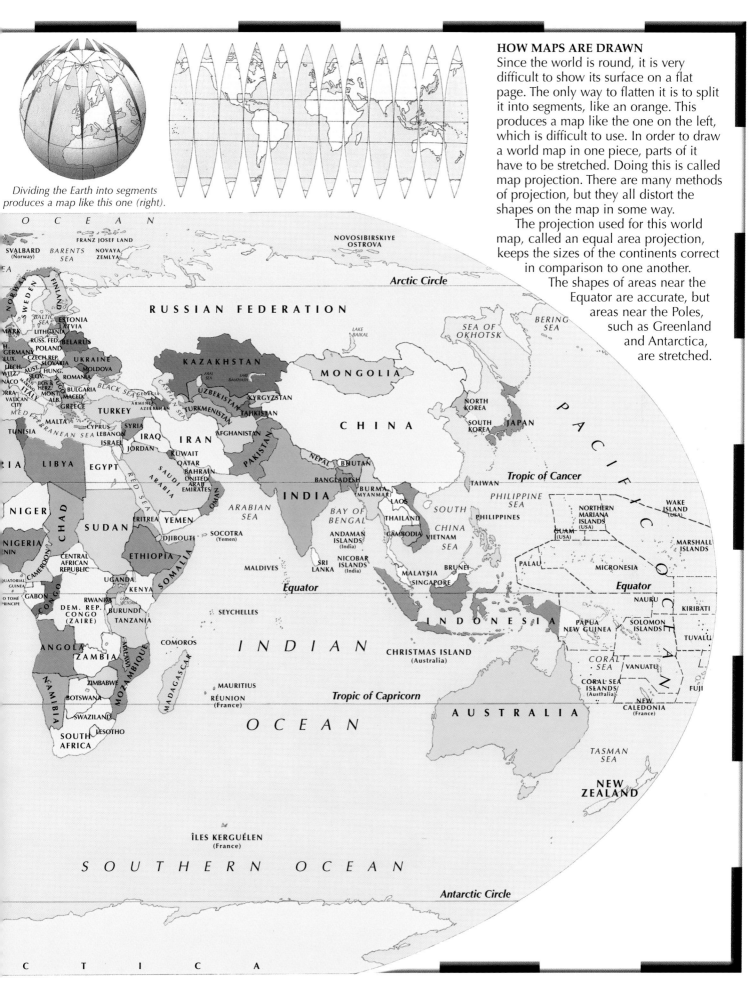

Dividing the Earth into segments produces a map like this one (right).

HOW MAPS ARE DRAWN

Since the world is round, it is very difficult to show its surface on a flat page. The only way to flatten it is to split it into segments, like an orange. This produces a map like the one on the left, which is difficult to use. In order to draw a world map in one piece, parts of it have to be stretched. Doing this is called map projection. There are many methods of projection, but they all distort the shapes on the map in some way.

The projection used for this world map, called an equal area projection, keeps the sizes of the continents correct in comparison to one another.

The shapes of areas near the Equator are accurate, but areas near the Poles, such as Greenland and Antarctica, are stretched.

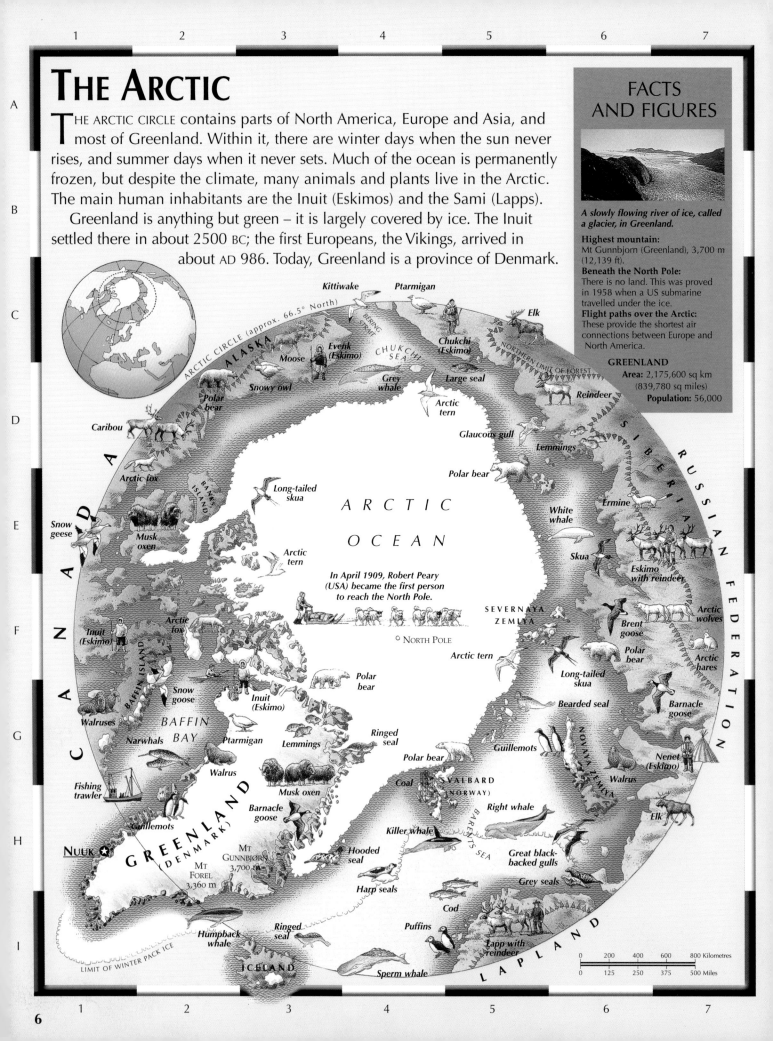

THE ARCTIC

THE ARCTIC CIRCLE contains parts of North America, Europe and Asia, and most of Greenland. Within it, there are winter days when the sun never rises, and summer days when it never sets. Much of the ocean is permanently frozen, but despite the climate, many animals and plants live in the Arctic. The main human inhabitants are the Inuit (Eskimos) and the Sami (Lapps).

Greenland is anything but green – it is largely covered by ice. The Inuit settled there in about 2500 BC; the first Europeans, the Vikings, arrived in about AD 986. Today, Greenland is a province of Denmark.

FACTS AND FIGURES

A slowly flowing river of ice, called a glacier, in Greenland.

Highest mountain:
Mt Gunnbjorn (Greenland), 3,700 m (12,139 ft).
Beneath the North Pole:
There is no land. This was proved in 1958 when a US submarine travelled under the ice.
Flight paths over the Arctic:
These provide the shortest air connections between Europe and North America.

GREENLAND
Area: 2,175,600 sq km (839,780 sq miles)
Population: 56,000

ARCTIC CIRCLE (approx. 66.5° North)

BERING STRAIT

CHUKCHI SEA

NORTHERN LIMIT OF FOREST

ALASKA

Kittiwake
Ptarmigan
Elk
Chukchi (Eskimo)
Evenk (Eskimo)
Moose
Snowy owl
Grey whale
Large seal
Arctic tern
Polar bear
Glaucous gull
Reindeer
Lemmings
Caribou
Polar bear
Arctic fox
White whale
Ermine
SIBERIAN
Snow geese
Musk oxen
BANKS ISLAND
Long-tailed skua
Arctic tern
Skua
Eskimo with reindeer
RUSSIAN FEDERATION

ARCTIC OCEAN

In April 1909, Robert Peary (USA) became the first person to reach the North Pole.

○ NORTH POLE

SEVERNAYA ZEMLYA
Arctic tern
Brent goose
Arctic wolves
Polar bear
Arctic hares
Inuit (Eskimo)
Arctic fox
Polar bear
Inuit (Eskimo)
Long-tailed skua
Barnacle goose
Bearded seal
Snow goose
BAFFIN ISLAND
Walruses
Narwhals
BAFFIN BAY
Ptarmigan
Lemmings
Ringed seal
Polar bear
Guillemots
NOVAYA ZEMLYA
Walrus
Nenet (Eskimo)
Fishing trawler
Walrus
Musk oxen
Coal
SVALBARD (NORWAY)
Right whale
BARENTS SEA
Elk
Barnacle goose
Killer whale
Guillemots
NUUK ★
GREENLAND (DENMARK)
MT GUNNBJØRN 3,700 m
MT FOREL 3,360 m
Hooded seal
Great black-backed gulls
Grey seals
Harp seals
Cod
Humpback whale
Ringed seal
Puffins
Lapp with reindeer
LIMIT OF WINTER PACK ICE
ICELAND
Sperm whale
LAPLAND

0 200 400 600 800 Kilometres
0 125 250 375 500 Miles

CANADA

THE ANTARCTIC

THE ANTARCTIC HAS the world's coldest climate. Nearly all the land is covered by ice about 2,000 m (6,562 ft) thick. In summer, the ice at the edge of the sheet breaks off to form icebergs. In winter, the sea at the edge of the sheet freezes again and is called pack ice. There are very few plants, and Antarctic animals such as seals depend on the sea for their food.

No country owns Antarctica, but a number claim territory, and many have research bases there. The world's coldest temperature of -89.2°C (-128.6°F) was recorded at Vostock Station in July 1983.

FACTS AND FIGURES

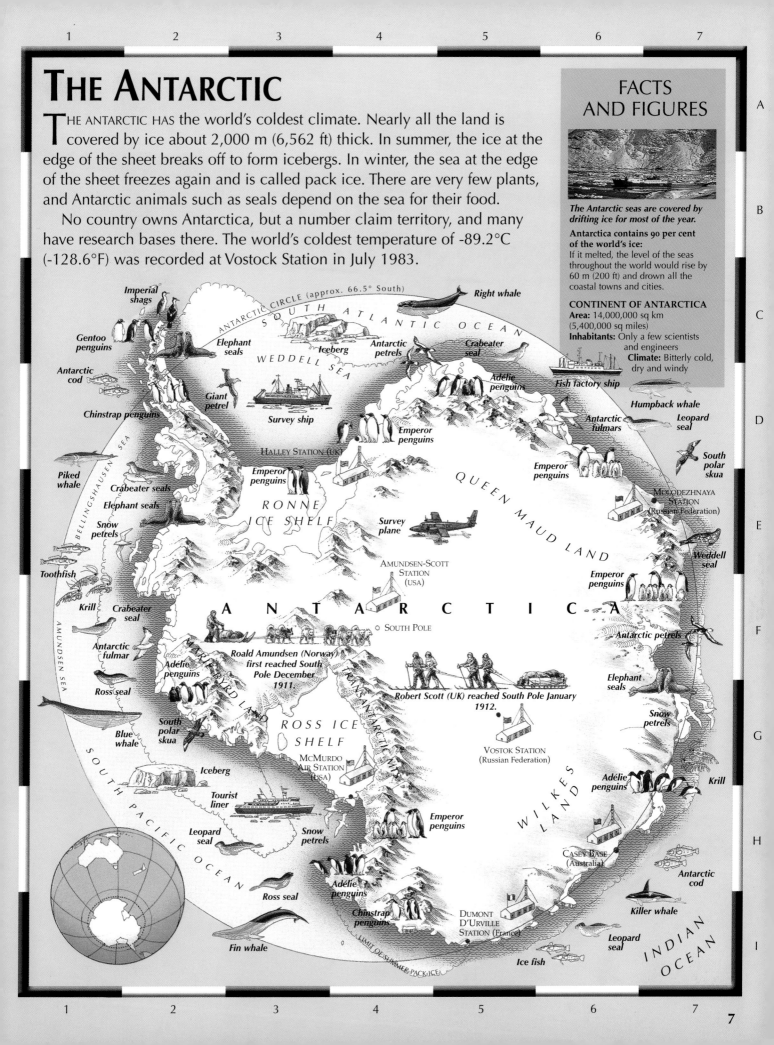

The Antarctic seas are covered by drifting ice for most of the year.

Antarctica contains 90 per cent of the world's ice: If it melted, the level of the seas throughout the world would rise by 60 m (200 ft) and drown all the coastal towns and cities.

CONTINENT OF ANTARCTICA
Area: 14,000,000 sq km (5,400,000 sq miles)
Inhabitants: Only a few scientists and engineers
Climate: Bitterly cold, dry and windy

THE BRITISH ISLES

THE BRITISH ISLES lie off the northwest coast of Europe. They consist of two large islands – Great Britain and Ireland – surrounded by smaller ones. The British Isles are divided into two countries: the United Kingdom and Ireland. The United Kingdom (UK), also known as Britain, is made up of England, Wales, Scotland, and Northern Ireland.

During the 18th and 19th centuries, the UK was the first country to undergo an industrial revolution. It became the world's leading manufacturing and trading nation and acquired a vast empire, including Canada, Australia, New Zealand, India, and much of Africa. During the 20th century, most of these colonies became independent, although they remain linked with Britain through the Commonwealth. Today, the United Kingdom is a member of the European Union.

Until the last century, all of Ireland was part of the UK. In 1921 southern Ireland, where most people are Roman Catholic, became an independent country, while the northern part of Ireland, where the people are mainly Protestant, remained British.

FACTS AND FIGURES

Much of Ireland's wealth comes from farming.

Largest metropolitan areas:
Dublin, 915,000; Cork, 174,400;
Limerick, 75,500
Highest mountain:
Carrauntoohil, 1,038 m (3,415 ft)
Longest river:
Shannon, 386 km (240 miles)

IRELAND
Capital: Dublin
Area: 70,284 sq km (27,136 sq miles)
Population: 3,700,000
Languages: English, Irish
Religion: Christian
Currency: Euro
Government: Multiparty Republic

FACTS AND FIGURES

The mountainous area of Snowdonia, in northern Wales, is traditionally popular for hill walking and mountaineering.

Largest cities:
London (Eng), 6,679,700;
Manchester (Eng), 2,775,000;
Birmingham (Eng), 2,551,700.
Highest mountains:
Ben Nevis (Scot), 1,343 m
(4,406 ft); Snowdon (Wales),
1,085 m (3,560 ft).
Longest rivers:
Severn (Eng–Wales), 354 km
(220 miles); Thames (Eng),
346 km (215 miles).

The parish church is the traditional centre of English country town and village life.

UNITED KINGDOM
Capital: London
Area: 244,017 sq km
(94,215 sq miles)
Population: 59,000,000
Language: English
Religion: Christian
Currency: Pound sterling
Government: Constitutional Monarchy

ENGLAND
Capital: London
Area: 130,360 sq km
(50,332 sq miles)
Population: 48,471,200

NORTHERN IRELAND
Capital: Belfast
Area: 14,121 sq km (5,452 sq miles)
Population: 1,943,400

SCOTLAND
Capital: Edinburgh
Area: 78,769 sq km (30,412 sq miles)
Population: 5,448,600

WALES
Capital: Cardiff
Area: 20,767 sq km (8,018 sq miles)
Population: 3,136,800

Map labels:

SHETLAND ISLANDS
Crofting (farming)
Lerwick
UNITED KINGDOM
Pilchards
ORKNEY ISLANDS
Seals
Cod
Haddock
Fish packing
Aberdeen
Oil rig
Highland dress
Fishing trawler
Newcastle
ISLE OF LEWIS
Harris tweed
OUTER HEBRIDES
NORTH UIST
SOUTH UIST
SKYE
Sheep
Red deer
Salmon
Whisky
BEN NEVIS 1,343 m
BALMORAL CASTLE
SCOTLAND
LOCH NESS MONSTER
LOCH LOMOND
Machinery
Edinburgh
EDINBURGH CASTLE
Golf
Sheep
Highland cattle
ISLE OF MULL
Glasgow
ISLE OF ARRAN
ISLAY
GIANT'S CAUSEWAY
Londonderry

MAP QUIZ

- ◆ Where was the poet and playwright William Shakespeare born?

- ◆ St George's Channel runs between which two countries?

- ◆ What river runs through Nottingham?

- ◆ The Vikings sailed to Ireland in wooden ships. Which Northern Irish city is famous for shipbuilding today?

- ◆ Name the two countries divided by Hadrian's wall, built by Roman soldiers.

- ◆ Can you find two castles in Scotland?

- ◆ Which British island plays host to an annual motorbike race?

- ◆ Which woollen fabric is woven on the Isle of Lewis in the Outer Hebrides?

FRANCE

FRANCE, ONE OF Europe's major farming and industrial nations, is famous for food and wine. The landscape varies dramatically from region to region and includes hot, dry areas, farmland, mountains, and forests.

France has always been powerful in Europe. In 1789 the people overthrew the king, Louis XVI, during what was later called the French Revolution. After the revolution, Napoleon, a general in the army, crowned himself Emperor. He went on to conquer most of Europe, but was defeated by the English at the Battle of Waterloo in 1815.

Today, France is a leading manufacturing country, with iron, steel, chemical, car, aeroplane, and textile industries. France is rich in farmland, and its major crops include oats, barley, wheat, flax, sugar beet, and grapes. Dairy farming is widespread and French farmers produce over 700 different types of cheese.

In terms of tourism, there are many coastal resorts, and the mountains are popular for winter sports.

MAP QUIZ

+ On which river would you find the town of Arles, with its Roman Amphitheatre?

+ The Pyrenees separate France from what other country?

+ Name the widely used condiment associated with the city of Dijon.

+ Which famous sparkling wine comes from northeastern France?

+ Can you find the site of thousands of prehistoric standing stones?

+ Which city on the edge of the Massif Central is best known for its porcelain industry?

+ On which sea are the resort towns of Nice and Cannes?

+ A winding river runs through the centre of Paris. Can you name it?

+ Pigs are used to hunt for a rare edible fungus. What is it?

+ Which city is a natural harbour at the mouth of the Seine river?

UNITED KINGDOM

CHANNEL TUNNEL

ENGLISH CHANNEL

ATLANTIC OCEAN

Tourism

Ferry

Pollock

Shellfish

Fishing

Le Havre

Seine

CHANNEL ISLANDS (UK)

Tourism

Artichokes

MONT ST MICHEL

BAYEUX TAPESTRY

Crab

Tourism

Calvados (apple brandy)

Dairy cattle

QUIMPER CATHEDRAL

Brest

Fishing

Breton head-dress

Rennes

Le Mans

Quimper

STANDING STONES (CARNAC)

TGV high-speed train

Tours

Loire

Warship

Loire

Nantes

CHÂTEAU DE CHENONCEAUX

Mackerel

Eels

FRANCE

Wine

Beef cattle

F   R

Oysters

Tourism

Fishing

Geese

Limog

BAY OF BISCAY

Sailing

Brandy

CAVE PAINTING (LASCAUX)

Gironde

Pine trees

Dordogne

Oysters

Bordeaux

Tobacco

Garonne

Pine trees

Wine

Agen

Windsurfing

Walnuts

Boules (French bowls)

Oil

Brown bear

Biarritz

Oil

Pau

Ibex (type of goat)

PYRENEES

S P A I N

0	50	100	150	200 Kilometres
0	25	50	75	100	125 Miles

BELGIUM

GERMANY

Dunkirk

Calais

Lille

WORLD WAR I MEMORIAL (VIMY)

AMIENS CATHEDRAL

niens

Beef cattle

ashion design

LUXEMBOURG

Coal

CHÂTEAU BAS (SEDAN)

Reims

Coal

Metz

Wine

Champagne

Potatoes

Nancy

Strasbourg

VOSGES

Storks

Cars

PARIS

CHÂTEAU DE PIERREFONDS

Wheat

Seine

Wild boar

Pigs

CHARTRES CATHEDRAL

Orléans

Wine

SAINTE MADELEINE (VÉZELAY)

Mustard

Dijon

CHAPEL OF NOTRE DAME DU HAUT (RONCHAMP)

Mulhouse

SWITZERLAND

CHÂTEAU DE HAMBORD

Beaune

Wine

Deer

CHÂTEAUNEUF (NIÈVRE)

Saône

ANCE

Loire

Porcelain

Mâcon

Rhône

Rhône

TGV high-speed train

MONT BLANC 4,807 M

ITALY

Hunting for truffles

Clermont-Ferrand

Lyon

St Etienne

Skiing

MASSIF CENTRAL

cling

CHAPEL OF ST MICHEL D'AIGUILHE (LE PUY)

Grenoble

Mountain climbing

CEVENNES

ALPS

Chamois (type of goat)

Snails

Wine

Sheep

T VALENTRE (CAHORS)

Olives

Tourism

Aircraft industry

ulouse

Montpellier

AMPHITHEATRE AT ARLES

Lavender

MONACO

Nice

Cannes

Tourism

MONACO

Garonne

Marseille

Tourism

Toulon

VALLED TOWN (CARCASSONNE)

Tourism

Flamingos

Fishing

Sailing

Warship

OLAR FURNACE (ODEILLO)

Wine

Sardines

MEDITERRANEAN SEA

FACTS AND FIGURES

Amboise is one of the many historic towns along the River Loire.

Highest mountains:
Mont Blanc, 4,807 m (15,770 ft);
Les Ecrins, 4,103 m (13,461 ft);
Pic de Vignemale, 3,298 m (10,820 ft);
Mont Dore, 1,886 m (6,188 ft).
Longest rivers:
Loire, 1,005 km (625 miles);
Rhône-Saône, 812 km (505 miles);
Seine, 775 km (481 miles).
Largest cities:
Paris, 9,318,900; Lyon, 1,262,300;
Marseille, 1,231,000; Lille, 959,300;
Bordeaux, 969,400

The high-speed TGV train, which runs between Paris and Lyon.

FRANCE
Capital: Paris
Area: 551,500 sq km
(212,936 sq miles)
Population: 59,000,000
Language: French
Religion: Christian
Currency: Euro

MONACO
Capital: Monaco
Area: 1.6 sq km (0.6 sq miles)
Population: 32,000
Language: French
Religion: Christian
Currency: Euro

Sunflowers are grown all over southern France.

CORSICA (France)

Bastia

Tourism

CORSICA

Ajaccio

Tourism

BELGIUM, THE NETHERLANDS, AND LUXEMBOURG

BELGIUM, THE NETHERLANDS, and Luxembourg are called the "Low Countries" because they lie on the flat, low North European Plain. Almost half the Netherlands is below sea level. The saying, "God made the world, but the Dutch made the Netherlands", refers to the land they reclaimed from the sea. These areas, called polders, were drained, then protected from floods with walls, or dykes.

Belgium, the Netherlands, and Luxembourg are often called "Benelux", a short version of their names. These small countries have large populations: the Netherlands has one of the highest concentrations of people in Europe – an average of 466 in each square kilometre. All three countries are industrial, but farming, fishing and tourism are also important. Belgium and the Netherlands have been trading nations for centuries, and today, Antwerp and Rotterdam are the two busiest ports in Europe.

The Benelux countries belong to the European Union based in Brussels. Luxembourg is a centre for European organizations, while the International Courts of Justice are situated at The Hague.

BELGIUM

R
E
G

BELGIUM

LUXEMBOURG

Chemicals

Maastricht

Iron and steel

Mt Botrange 694 m

Wild boar

CLERVAUX

Liège

Apples

Deer

Crystal

LOUVAIN TOWN HALL

Meuse

A R D E N N E S

L U X E M B O U R G

Wine

Namur

WALZIN

LUXEMBOURG

BRUSSELS

Charleroi

Pigs

Esch-sur-Alzette

Chocolates

Sambre

EU HEADQUARTERS

Iron and steel

Mons

Vegetables

Oudenaarde

Beef cattle

Tournai

Kortrijk

TOURNAI CATHEDRAL

Beer

F   R   A   N   C   E

MAP QUIZ

✦ Which country has the same name as its capital city?

✦ What modern Dutch city is famous for the manufacture of electronic equipment and appliances?

✦ Where would you find an international centre for the cutting and selling of diamonds?

✦ The Ardennes Mountains completely cover one of the Benelux countries. Which one is it?

✦ Name the Belgian city known for both its medieval stone buildings and the exquisite lace produced there.

✦ Some of the finest chocolate in the world is exported from this region. Which country is responsible?

✦ Can you find the headquarters of the European Union?

✦ What pretty blue-and-white pottery has been manufactured in the Netherlands for hundreds of years?

FACTS AND FIGURES

BELGIUM
Capital: Brussels
Area: 30,514 sq km (11,781 sq miles)
Population: 10,200,000
Languages: French, Dutch, some German
Religion: Christian
Currency: Euro

LUXEMBOURG
Capital: Luxembourg
Area: 2,586 sq km (998 sq miles)
Population: 431,000
Languages: Letzeburgesch, French, German
Religion: Christian
Currencies: Euro

NETHERLANDS
Capital: Amsterdam
Seat of government: The Hague
Area: 40,844 sq km (15,770 sq miles)
Population: 15,800,000
Language: Dutch
Religion: Christian
Currency: Euro

The historic Belgian city of Bruges is famous for its lace.

Highest mountain:
Mt Botrange (Belg), 694 m (2,277 ft).
Lowest point:
Prins Alexander Polder (Neth), 6.7 m (22 ft) below sea level.
Largest cities:
Brussels (Belg), 950,400;
Amsterdam (Neth) 1,091,400;
Rotterdam (Neth), 1,069,400;
The Hague (Neth), 694,400

Rotterdam in the Netherlands is a major international port.

80 Kilometres
50 Miles
0 10 20 30 40 50 60
0   20   40   60   80

SCANDINAVIA

SCANDINAVIA CONSISTS OF Denmark, Norway, Sweden, and Finland in northern Europe, and the island of Iceland in the North Atlantic. Denmark is low lying farmland, whereas most of Norway is mountainous with coastal bays called fjords. Finland is full of forests and lakes, while Sweden has a varied landscape that includes forest, farmland, mountains and lakes. Central Iceland is a plateau of volcanoes, lava fields and glaciers, so most people live near the coast. Scandinavia has important natural resources, including timber, fish, iron ore and oil and natural gas in the North Sea. Today, the Scandinavian countries are all industrial, and their people enjoy a high standard of living.

MAP QUIZ

✦ Lego building blocks were invented in which Scandinavian country, where there is a theme park dedicated to them?

✦ Where would you see the statue of the Little Mermaid?

✦ Can you identify two Scandinavian countries that have large paper-making industries?

✦ Name a region where you can find reindeer like the ones associated with the legend of Father Christmas.

✦ In which country are Volvo cars manufactured?

✦ A large mountain range runs along the border between Norway and Sweden. What is it called?

NORWAY

NORWEGIAN SEA

ATLANTIC OCEAN

Fishing trawler

Salmon

Coastal express

Trondheim

Skiing

STAVE CHURCH (BORGUND)

Wolverine

GALDHØPIGGEN 2,469 m

Mountain climbing

Bergen

CITY HALL (OSLO)

Ski jumping

Electric power

Stavanger

Folk costume

OSLO

Paper

Oil and gas

Sheep

Sheep

Herrings

SKAGERRAK

STATUE OF POSEIDON

Karlstad

LAKE VÄNERN

LA VÄTT

Borås

ICELAND

Puffins

Sheep

GODAFOSS WATERFALL

VATNAJÖKULL (ICE SHEET)

Herrings

STROKKUR GEYSER

REYKJAVIK

Cod

ICELAND

DENMARK

NORTH SEA

Gothenburg

Volvo cars

Dairy cattle

KRONBORG CAS HELSINGOR

LEGOLAND

Legoland

Aarhus

DENMARK

Esbjerg

COPENHAGEN

Malmö

Pigs

LITTLE MERMAID STATUE (COPENHAGEN)

GERMANY

KATTEGAT

NORTH CAPE

BARENTS SEA

Fishing trawler

Reindeer

Tromso

Cod

LOFOTEN ISLANDS

VESTERÅLEN

Puffins

Narvik

Sami (Lapps)

LAPLAND

Wolves

Iron ore

Salmon

Elk

Birch tree

Lynx

Cross-country skiing

Sailing

Sauna

Oulu

Norway spruce

Furs

Umeå

Scots pine

Salmon

GULF OF BOTHNIA

Folk costume

TAMPERE CATHEDRAL

Paper

Herrings

Model horse (Dalarna)

Tampere

Trout

DROTTINGHOLM PALACE

Lahti

HELSINKI RAILWAY STATION

Potatoes

Turku

rebro

Uppsala

ÅLAND ISLANDS

HELSINKI

STOCKHOLM

GULF OF FINLAND

CITY HALL (STOCKHOLM)

Ice-breaker ship

ESTONIA

Rune stone (ancient inscription)

GOTLAND

BALTIC SEA

ÖLAND

Guillemots

LATVIA

RUSSIAN FEDERATION

FINLAND

SWEDEN

FACTS AND FIGURES

Scandinavia's forests support large timber and paper industries.

Highest mountain:
Galdhøpiggen (Norway), 2,469 m (8,100 ft).

Largest lake:
Lake Vänern (Sweden), 5,580 sq km (2,155 sq miles).

Largest cities:
Copenhagen (Denmark), 1,342,700;
Stockholm (Sweden), 1,450,000;
Helsinki (Finland), 1,040,000;
Oslo (Norway) 720,000;
Gothenborg (Sweden) 710,900

Copenhagen has been a port and trading centre since the Middle Ages.

DENMARK
Capital: Copenhagen
Area: 43,077 sq km (16,632 sq miles)
Population: 5,300,000
Language: Danish
Religion: Christian
Currency: Danish krone
Government: Constitutional Monarchy

FINLAND
Capital: Helsinki
Area: 338,127 sq km (130,551 sq miles)
Population: 5,200,000
Languages: Finnish, Swedish, Lappish
Religion: Christian
Currency: Euro
Government: Multiparty Republic

ICELAND
Capital: Reykjavik
Area: 103,000 sq km (39,768 sq miles)
Population: 281,000
Language: Icelandic
Religion: Christian
Currency: Icelandic krona
Government: Constitutional Republic

NORWAY
Capital: Oslo
Area: 323,895 sq km (125,056 sq miles)
Population: 4,500,000
Languages: Norwegian, Lappish
Religion: Christian
Currency: Norwegian krona
Government: Constitutional Monarchy

SWEDEN
Capital: Stockholm
Area: 440,945 sq km (170,250 sq miles)
Population: 8,900,000
Languages: Swedish, Lappish
Religion: Christian
Currency: Swedish krone
Government: Constitutional Monarchy

0 50 100 150 200 250 Kilometres

0 50 100 150 Miles

GERMANY, AUSTRIA, AND SWITZERLAND

THE LANDSCAPE IN this region is crossed by two of Europe's longest rivers: the Rhine, flowing north to the North Sea, and the Danube, flowing east to the Black Sea.

For hundreds of years, the area now called Germany consisted of small independent states, which were first united in 1871. Germany rapidly became an important power, but after World War II, the country was split into two parts: the Federal Republic of Germany (West Germany) and the communist German Democratic Republic (East Germany). This split lasted for over 40 years. The two German states were reunited in 1990, following the collapse of communism in East Germany. Today, Germany is the wealthiest country in Europe and one of the world's foremost industrial nations.

To the south lie the mountainous countries of Austria and Switzerland, which both rely heavily on tourism. Switzerland is famous for watches and scientific instruments, and it is also a major business centre. Becoming neutral in 1815, it has stayed out of every war affecting Europe since then. Austria is also neutral. The tiny country of Liechtenstein is only about 24 km (15 miles) long and 8 km (5 miles) wide.

| 0 | 50 | 100 | 150 | 200 Kilometres |
| 0 | 25 | 50 | 75 | 100 | 125 Miles |

The Alps

| EIGER | MÖNCH | JUNGFRAU |
| 3,970 m | 4,099 m | 4,158 m |

The Alps are the longest and highest mountain range in western Europe. They stretch from southeastern France, through Italy, Switzerland, Austria, Slovenia, and Croatia, into Yugoslavia – a distance of about 1,200 km (750 miles). People from around the world visit the Alps to take part in sports such as skiing and mountaineering.

NORTH SEA

DENMARK

Pigs · Sailing · Cod · Kiel · KIEL CANAL · Shipbuilding · Lübeck · Hamburg · Electronics · Potatoes · Tourism · Elbe · Bremerhaven · Bremen · Weser · Dairy cattle · BREMEN CATHEDRAL · Beef cattle · LÜNEBURG HEATH · Wheat · Sausages · Hannover · HANNOVER TO... HA... · Iron and steel · Machinery · Volkswagen cars · Coal · Lippe · Essen · Dortmund · Sugar beet · Düsseldorf · Ruhr · COLOGNE CATHEDRAL · Kassel · Chemicals · Cologne · GERMAN... · Erfu... · Bonn · Potatoes · Strip-mining coal · Frankfurt skyline · Wheat · BEETHOVEN'S BIRTHPLACE · Wiesbaden · Lebkuch... biscuits · THE LORELEI ROCK · Frankfurt am Main · Mainz · Main · Wine · Nureml... · Mannheim · Wine · ROTHENBURG TOWN HALL · Traditional Bavarian costume · Coal · Saarbrücken · FRANCE · Stuttgart · Danub... · Cuckoo clocks · Mercedes-Benz cars · ULM CATHEDRAL · NEUSCHWANSTEIN CASTLE · LIECHTENSTEIN · SWITZERLAND · Rhine · Freiburg im Breisgau · HOHENZOLLERN CASTLE · LAKE CONSTANCE · Watches · Traditional Swiss costume · VADUZ · Innsbru... · Gruyère cheese · Basel · Zürich · LIECHTENSTEIN · BERN · Dairy cattle · SWITZERLAND · Lausanne · Marmo... · LAKE GENEVA · Chocolate · Geneva · Skiing · Alpine horns · I · T · MATTERHORN 4,478 m

NETHERLANDS · BELGIUM · LUXEMBOURG · Rhine

BALTIC SEA

RÜGEN

Shipbuilding

Rostock
Storks

Sheep

chwerin

Sugar beet

GERMANY

Dairy cattle

BRANDENBURG GATE

Machinery

★ BERLIN

Potsdam

Magdeburg

Pigs

Poultry

Halle

Leipzig

Y

Elbe

Strip-mining coal

Textiles
Dresden

Chemnitz

Zwickau

Iron and steel

ZWINGER PALACE

P O L A N D

C Z E C H
R E P U B L I C

REGENSBURG CATHEDRAL

Regensburg

Beer

Sugar beet

Electronics

Munich

Linz

Danube

HOHENSALZBURG CASTLE

Salzburg

MOZART'S BIRTHPLACE

Violins

S   A U S T R I A

Edelweiss

Chamois (type of goat)

Mountain climbing

Skiing

Graz

Cakes

Lipizzaner horses

VIENNA OPERA HOUSE

★ VIENNA

Iron and steel

Dairy cattle

Great white heron

MARIA-HILF-KIRCHE (GRAZ)

AUSTRIA

A L Y

S L O V E N I A

S L O V A K I A

H U N G A R Y

FACTS AND FIGURES

Vienna's Belvedere Castle was built for the Habsburg family.

Longest rivers:
Danube, 2,858 km (1,776 miles); Rhine, 1,320 km (820 miles).

Largest lakes:
Lake Geneva (Switz-Fr), 580 sq km (224 sq miles); Lake Constance (Ger-Switz-Aust), 539 sq km (208 sq miles).

Largest cities:
Berlin (Ger), 3,446,000; Hamburg (Ger), 1,660,700; Vienna (Aust), 1,539,900; Munich (Ger), 1,236,500; Zurich (Switz), 1,158,100;, Cologne (Ger), 955,500; Frankfurt (Ger), 647,200; Essen (Ger), 626,100.

World's tallest spire:
The cathedral of Ulm in Germany has the world's tallest church spire. It is 161 m (528 ft) high.

Busiest canal:
Germany's Kiel Canal is the busiest in the world. Every year, about 45,000 ships use it to pass between the North Sea and the Baltic Sea.

World's longest road tunnel:
St Gotthard tunnel in Switzerland runs under the Alps, and is 16.32 km (10.14 miles) long.

World's biggest roof:
The glass roof over the Olympic Stadium in Munich measures 85,000 sq m (914,940 sq ft).

Cows grazing in the Alps give milk for Swiss chocolate.

AUSTRIA
Capital: Vienna
Area: 83,853 sq km (32,375 sq miles)
Population: 8,200,000
Language: German
Religion: Christian
Currency: Euro
Government: Multiparty Republic

GERMANY
Capital: Berlin
Area: 356,910 sq km (137,804 sq miles)
Population: 82,200,000
Language: German
Religion: Christian
Currency: Euro
Government: Multiparty Republic

LIECHTENSTEIN
Capital: Vaduz
Area: 160 sq km (62 sq miles)
Population: 32,000
Language: German
Religion: Christian
Currency: Swiss franc
Government: Constititional Monarchy

SWITZERLAND
Capital: Bern
Area: 41,293 sq km (15,943 sq miles)
Population: 7,400,000
Languages: German, French, Italian
Religion: Christian
Currency: Swiss franc
Government: Federal Republic

MAP QUIZ

✦ What mountain range extends across Germany, Austria and Switzerland?

✦ By which river would you find the Lorelei Rock, where a legendary water nymph lured sailors to their death?

✦ The birthplace of Wolfgang Amadeus Mozart is now the home of an important music festival. Which city is it?

✦ Name two important car manufacturers that are based in Germany.

✦ Which city is famous for its Opera House, its rich cakes and its elegant Lipizzaner horses?

✦ In which country would you be able to hear the distinctive sound of alpine horns?

✦ List four German cities that have beautiful old cathedrals shown on the map.

✦ Identify the country most closely associated with the white edelweiss flower.

✦ Where is the huge Matterhorn mountain?

SPAIN AND PORTUGAL

THE COUNTRIES OF Spain and Portugal occupy the Iberian Peninsula, which also contains the tiny independent state of Andorra and the British colony of Gibraltar.

Over time, Spain and Portugal have been invaded by many peoples, including the Romans and the Moors – Arabs from North Africa who ruled much of Spain for hundreds of years. Both countries have a long history of exploration: Columbus sailed from Spain to America in 1492, and in 1497, the Portuguese adventurer Vasco da Gama sailed around Africa to India for the first time. Settlers followed explorers, and by the 16th century Spain and Portugal had empires in North and South America, Asia, and Africa.

Today, many people make their living from farming or fishing, or in industry. Tourism is a major source of wealth in both countries.

PORTUGAL

MAP QUIZ

✦ Lisbon, the Portuguese capital, lies at the mouth of which river?

✦ Where would you go to see the annual event known as Running with the Bulls?

✦ In which Spanish city would you find the House of Shells?

✦ Portugal and Spain each have their own fortified wine. Can you name them?

✦ Find the Spanish town that is known for its prehistoric cave paintings.

✦ Which city, also famous for guitars, has a Roman aqueduct?

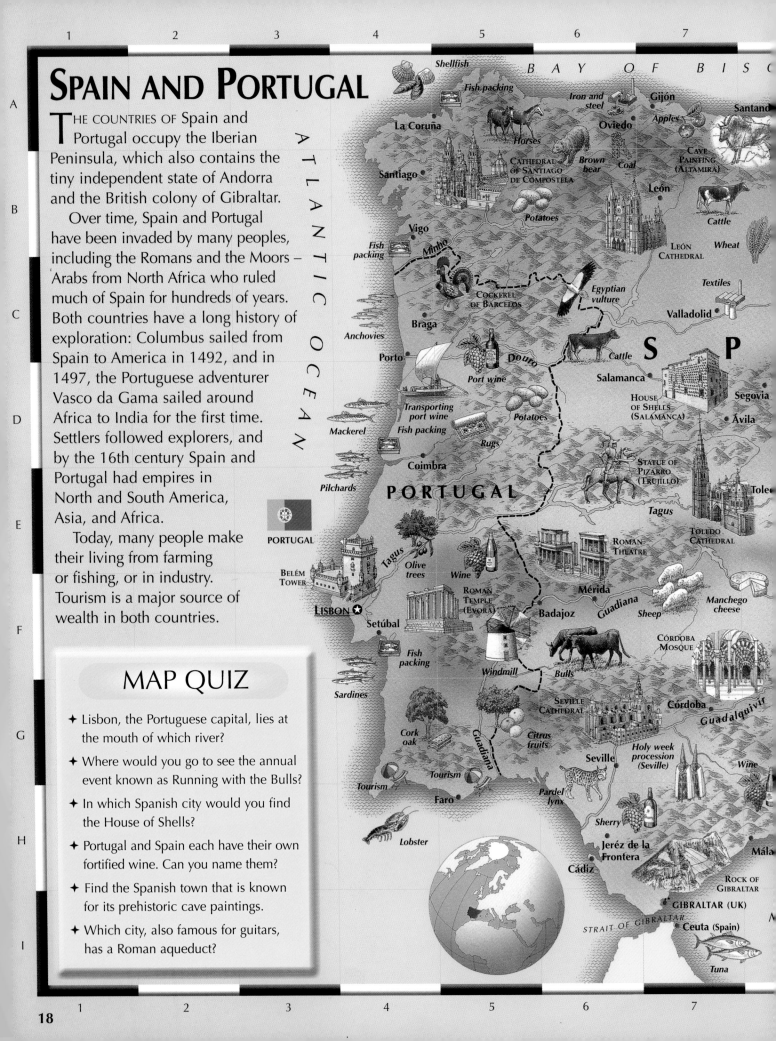

BAY OF BISC

Shellfish
Fish packing
Iron and steel
Gijón
La Coruña
Horses
Oviedo
Apples
Santand
Santiago
CATHEDRAL OF SANTIAGO DE COMPOSTELA
Brown bear
Coal
CAVE PAINTING (ALTAMIRA)
León
Vigo
Potatoes
Cattle
ATLANTIC OCEAN
Fish packing
Minho
LEÓN CATHEDRAL
Wheat
Braga
COCKEREL OF BARCELOS
Egyptian vulture
Textiles
Anchovies
Valladolid
Porto
Douro
Cattle
S P
Port wine
Salamanca
HOUSE OF SHELLS (SALAMANCA)
Segovia
Mackerel
Transporting port wine
Potatoes
Ávila
Fish packing
Rugs
STATUE OF PIZARRO (TRUJILLO)
Coimbra
Tagus
Tole
Pilchards
PORTUGAL
TOLEDO CATHEDRAL
Olive trees
ROMAN THEATRE
Tagus
BELÉM TOWER
Wine
Manchego cheese
ROMAN TEMPLE (ÉVORA)
Mérida
LISBON
Badajoz
Guadiana
Sheep
Setúbal
CÓRDOBA MOSQUE
Windmill
Bulls
Fish packing
SEVILLE CATHEDRAL
Córdoba
Guadalquivir
Sardines
Cork oak
Guadiana
Citrus fruits
Holy week procession (Seville)
Wine
Tourism
Seville
Tourism
Pardel lynx
Faro
Sherry
Lobster
Jeréz de la Frontera
Mála
Cádiz
ROCK OF GIBRALTAR
GIBRALTAR (UK)
STRAIT OF GIBRALTAR
Ceuta (Spain)
Tuna

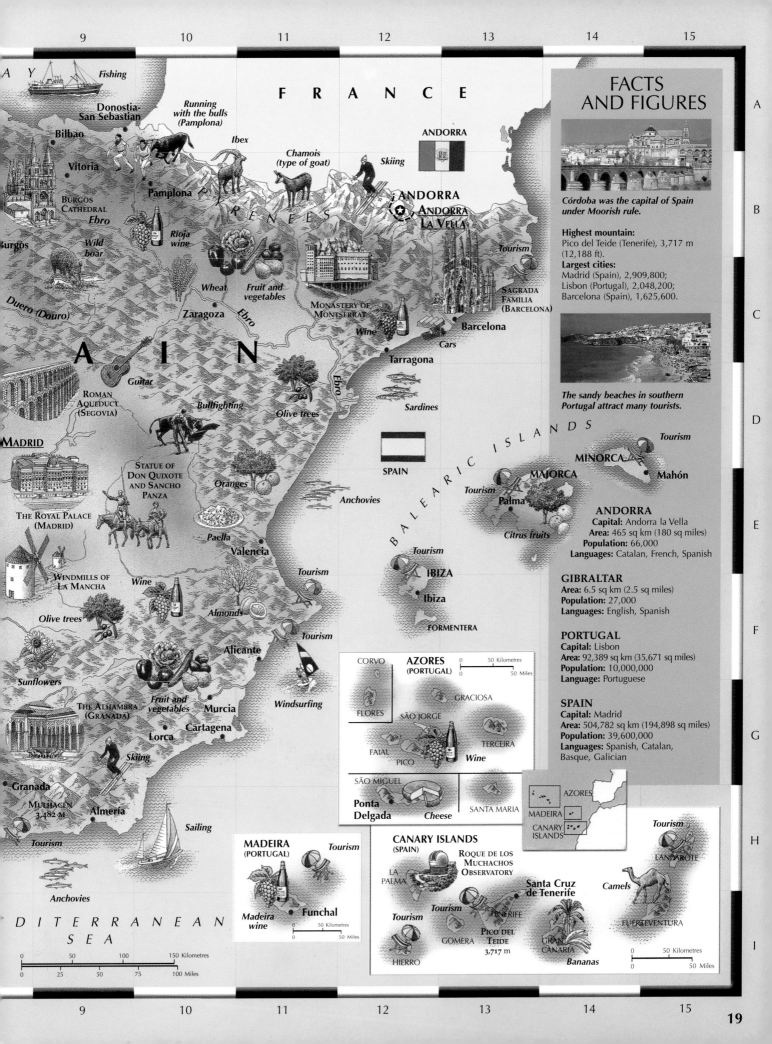

FRANCE

ANDORRA

Fishing

Donostia-San Sebastian

Bilbao

Vitoria

Burgos

BURGOS CATHEDRAL

Ebro

Duero (Douro)

Wild boar

Running with the bulls (Pamplona)

Ibex

Chamois (type of goat)

Skiing

Pamplona

PYRENEES

Rioja wine

Wheat

Fruit and vegetables

ANDORRA

ANDORRA LA VELLA

Tourism

MONASTERY OF MONTSERRAT

SAGRADA FAMILIA (BARCELONA)

Zaragoza

Ebro

Wine

Barcelona

Cars

Tarragona

S P A I N

Guitar

ROMAN AQUEDUCT (SEGOVIA)

Bullfighting

Olive trees

Ebro

Sardines

SPAIN

BALEARIC ISLANDS

MADRID

STATUE OF DON QUIXOTE AND SANCHO PANZA

THE ROYAL PALACE (MADRID)

Oranges

Anchovies

Tourism

MINORCA

Mahón

MAJORCA

Palma

Citrus fruits

WINDMILLS OF LA MANCHA

Paella

Valencia

Wine

Tourism

Tourism

IBIZA

Ibiza

FORMENTERA

Olive trees

Almonds

Tourism

Alicante

Windsurfing

Sunflowers

THE ALHAMBRA (GRANADA)

Fruit and vegetables

Murcia

Cartagena

Lorca

Skiing

Granada

MULHACÉN 3,482 m

Almería

Sailing

Tourism

Anchovies

M E D I T E R R A N E A N   S E A

FACTS AND FIGURES

Córdoba was the capital of Spain under Moorish rule.

Highest mountain:
Pico del Teide (Tenerife), 3,717 m (12,188 ft).
Largest cities:
Madrid (Spain), 2,909,800;
Lisbon (Portugal), 2,048,200;
Barcelona (Spain), 1,625,600.

The sandy beaches in southern Portugal attract many tourists.

Tourism

ANDORRA
Capital: Andorra la Vella
Area: 465 sq km (180 sq miles)
Population: 66,000
Languages: Catalan, French, Spanish

GIBRALTAR
Area: 6.5 sq km (2.5 sq miles)
Population: 27,000
Languages: English, Spanish

PORTUGAL
Capital: Lisbon
Area: 92,389 sq km (35,671 sq miles)
Population: 10,000,000
Language: Portuguese

SPAIN
Capital: Madrid
Area: 504,782 sq km (194,898 sq miles)
Population: 39,600,000
Languages: Spanish, Catalan, Basque, Galician

AZORES (PORTUGAL)
0　50 Kilometres
0　50 Miles
CORVO
FLORES
GRACIOSA
SÃO JORGE
FAIAL
PICO
TERCEIRA
Wine
SÃO MIGUEL
Ponta Delgada
Cheese
SANTA MARIA

AZORES
MADEIRA
CANARY ISLANDS

MADEIRA (PORTUGAL)
Tourism
Madeira wine
Funchal
0　50 Kilometres
0　50 Miles

CANARY ISLANDS (SPAIN)
ROQUE DE LOS MUCHACHOS OBSERVATORY
LA PALMA
Santa Cruz de Tenerife
Tourism
Camels
LANZAROTE
Tourism
TENERIFE
GOMERA
Pico del Teide 3,717 m
GRAN CANARIA
Bananas
HIERRO
FUERTEVENTURA
0　50 Kilometres
0　50 Miles

0　50　100　150 Kilometres
0　25　50　75　100 Miles

ITALY

The EASILY RECOGNIZABLE boot shape of Italy is a 800-km (500-mile) long peninsula that stretches south into the Mediterranean Sea. Most of the country is mountainous or hilly, and in the north, the Alps form a barrier between Italy and the rest of Europe. Running down the spine of the country are the Apennines, rugged mountains dotted with villages and towns that haven't changed for centuries. The Mediterranean islands of Sicily and Sardinia are also part of Italy.

Modern Italy, with Rome as its capital, only came into existence in 1870. Before then, the area was a patchwork of independent city states, and these states can still be seen today in Italy's 20 "regions". Two have remained independent – the Vatican City in Rome and the Republic of San Marino in northeastern Italy.

In Roman times, the Italian peninsula was the centre of a great empire, and the remains of Roman roads and buildings can still be seen. In the 14th-16th centuries, Italy was the centre of an important artistic movement called the Renaissance. Many beautiful paintings, sculptures, buildings, and poems were produced here, and among Italy's most famous Renaissance artists and writers were Michelangelo, Leonardo da Vinci, Raphael, and Dante. Today, millions of tourists each year visit Italy's ancient cities and art treasures.

Modern Italy has large steel, chemical, textile, and car industries, and farming is still important: wheat, corn, rice, grapes and olives are the main crops. Fishing plays a part too, with fresh seafood coming into many small coastal ports.

FACTS AND FIGURES

Venice is built on islands and has many canals in place of streets.

ITALY
Capital: Rome
Area: 301,268 sq km (116,320 sq miles)
Population: 57,300,000
Language: Italian
Religion: Christian
Currency: Euro
Government: Multiparty Republic

MALTA
Capital: Valletta
Area: 316 sq km (122 sq miles)
Population: 389,000
Languages: Maltese, English
Religion: Christian
Currency: Maltese Lira
Government: Multiparty Republic

SAN MARINO
Capital: San Marino
Area: 61 sq km (23 sq miles)
Population: 26,000
Language: Italian
Religion: Christian
Currency: Euro
Government: Multiparty Republic

VATICAN CITY
Area: 0.44 sq km (0.17 sq miles)
Population: 1,000

A horse race called the Palio takes place in Siena each year.

Highest mountains:
Mont Blanc (It-Fr), 4,807 m (15,770 ft); Monte Rosa (It-Switz), 4,634 m (15,203 ft).

Longest river:
Po, 672 km (418 miles).

Largest lakes:
Lake Garda, 370 sq km (143 sq miles); Lake Maggiore, 212 sq km (82 sq miles); Lake Como, 145 sq km (55 sq miles).

Largest cities:
Milan, 3,750,000; Rome, 3,175,000; Naples, 2,875,000; Turin, 1,550,000.

ADRIATIC SEA

Crabs

Wine

Brindisi

Bari

Taranto

Oysters

CASTEL DEL MONTE

Octopus

Steel

Citrus fruits

Olive trees

Crotone

BRONZES OF RIACE

Sea bream

Red mullet

Tobacco

Foggia

Almonds

APENNINES

VESUVIUS 1,277 m

Salerno

Goats

Temple of Paestum

Reggio di Calabria

Garfish

Anchovies

Messina

Tourism

Mt. Etna 3,323 m

I T A L Y

THE COLOSSEUM (ROME)

Naples

Tourism

CAPRI

ISCHIA

Prawns

STROMBOLI

AEOLIAN ISLANDS

Syracuse

Carob tree

Ragusa

Pescara

Pasta

Tiber

Pizza

Shellfish

Swordfish

Citrus fruits

Palermo

Agrigento

S I C I L Y

ROME ★

VATICAN CITY

Wine

GIGLIO

Ferry boat

USTICA

TEMPLE OF CASTOR AND POLLOX

Wine

GOZO

★ **VALLETTA**

M A L T A

I O N I A N   S E A

ELBA

Grey mullet

Scuba diving

Tourism

Tuna

T Y R R H E N I A N   S E A

Sardines

PANTELLERIA

M E D I T E R R A N E A N   S E A

CORSICA

Crayfish

Petro-chemicals

Olive trees

Goats and sheep

SARDINIA

Citrus fruits

Cagliari

Tourism

Wine

150 Kilometres

100 Miles

0   25   50   75   100   125

0   50   100   150

MALTA

SAN MARINO

VATICAN CITY

ITALY

MAP QUIZ

◆ Where would you find the live volcano of Mount Etna?

◆ Name the five seas that surround Italy.

◆ Which river runs through Florence?

◆ In what city are Fiat cars manufactured?

◆ Which Italian island gave its name to a small fish that lives in the surrounding waters?

◆ Gladiators once fought to the death in the Colosseum. Where is it?

◆ Which city in the Alps shares its name with the lake it lies on?

CENTRAL AND EASTERN EUROPE

THIS REGION HAS ALWAYS been subject to change, and the borders have shifted many times. After World War II, all the countries apart from Greece became part of the "Eastern Bloc". They had communist regimes and ties with the former USSR. In recent years, however, many nations have established democratic governments with links to Western Europe.

The north of the region is dominated by Poland, which is rich in coal and copper, with large iron, steel, shipbuilding and textile industries. Farming is also important: the main crops are potatoes, wheat, and sugar beet.

To the south lie the Czech Republic and Slovakia, which until 1993 were one country – Czechoslovakia – with two peoples (Czechs and Slovaks) speaking different languages.

Below this is southeastern Europe: Greece, Albania, Bosnia and Herzegovina, Croatia, Slovenia, Macedonia, Yugoslavia, Bulgaria, Romania, and Hungary. Many of these countries were only formed at the end of the two World Wars. More recently, the republics of Bosnia and Herzegovina, Croatia, Macedonia and Slovenia broke away from Yugoslavia and were recognized as independent countries.

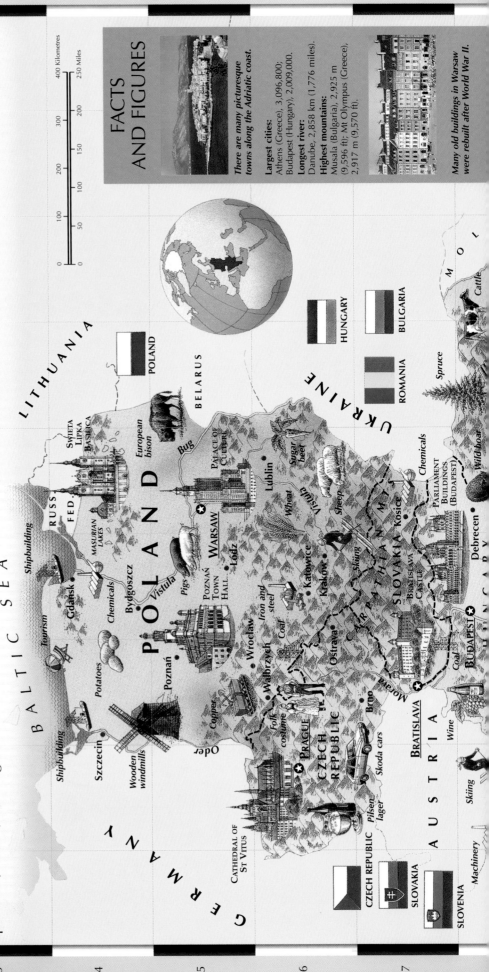

FACTS AND FIGURES

There are many picturesque towns along the Adriatic coast.

Largest cities: Athens (Greece), 3,096,800; Budapest (Hungary), 2,009,000.
Longest river: Danube, 2,858 km (1,776 miles).
Highest mountains: Musala (Bulgaria), 2,925 m (9,596 ft); Mt Olympus (Greece), 2,917 m (9,570 ft).

Many old buildings in Warsaw were rebuilt after World War II.

400 Kilometres
250 Miles

POLAND

HUNGARY

BULGARIA

ROMANIA

CZECH REPUBLIC

SLOVAKIA

SLOVENIA

LITHUANIA

BELARUS

RUSS. FED.

UKRAINE

BALTIC SEA

Shipbuilding

Tourism

Gdansk

Szczecin

Shipbuilding

Wooden windmills

Oder

Potatoes

Poznań

Chemicals

Bydgoszcz

Vistula

Pigs

POZNAŃ TOWN HALL

Wrocław

POLAND

ŚWIĘTA LIPKA BASILICA

MASURIAN LAKES

European bison

Bug

PALACE OF CULTURE

WARSAW

Łódź

Lublin

Wheat

Sugar beet

Vistula

Sheep

Skiing

CARPATHIAN MTS

Košice

SLOVAKIA

Chemicals

PARLIAMENT BUILDINGS (BUDAPEST)

Wild boar

Spruce

MOL

Cattle

Katowice

Kraków

Iron and steel

Wałbrzych

Coal

Ostrava

Copper

Folk costume

Brno

Morava

BRATISLAVA CASTLE

BRATISLAVA

Wine

Coal

BUDAPEST

HUNGARY

Debrecen

Škoda cars

PRAGUE

CZECH REPUBLIC

CATHEDRAL OF ST VITUS

Plzeň lager

AUSTRIA

Skiing

Machinery

GERMANY

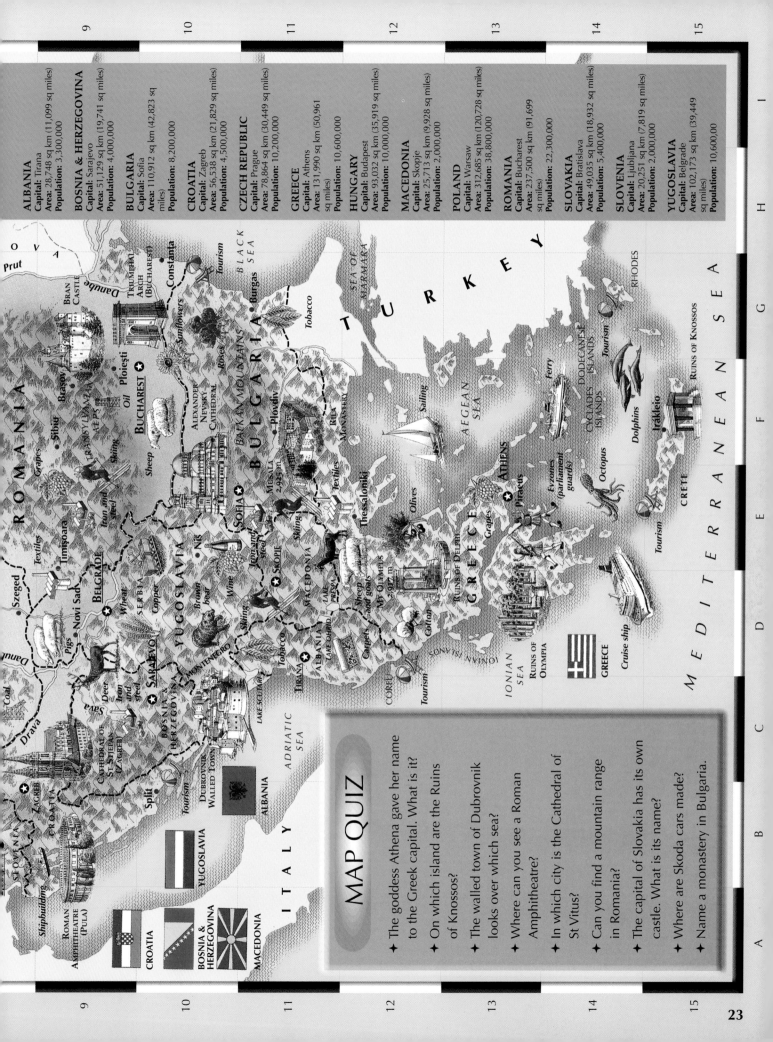

ALBANIA
Capital: Tirana
Area: 28,748 sq km (11,099 sq miles)
Population: 3,300,000

BOSNIA & HERZEGOVINA
Capital: Sarajevo
Area: 51,129 sq km (19,741 sq miles)
Population: 4,000,000

BULGARIA
Capital: Sofia
Area: 110,912 sq km 42,823 sq miles)
Population: 8,200,000

CROATIA
Capital: Zagreb
Area: 56,538 sq km (21,829 sq miles)
Population: 4,500,000

CZECH REPUBLIC
Capital: Prague
Area: 78,864 sq km (30,449 sq miles)
Population: 10,200,000

GREECE
Capital: Athens
Area: 131,990 sq km (50,961 sq miles)
Population: 10,600,000

HUNGARY
Capital: Budapest
Area: 93,032 sq km (35,919 sq miles)
Population: 10,000,000

MACEDONIA
Capital: Skopje
Area: 25,713 sq km (9,928 sq miles)
Population: 2,000,000

POLAND
Capital: Warsaw
Area: 312,685 sq km (120,728 sq miles)
Population: 38,800,000

ROMANIA
Capital: Bucharest
Area: 237,500 sq km (91,699 sq miles)
Population: 22,300,000

SLOVAKIA
Capital: Bratislava
Area: 49,035 sq km (18,932 sq miles)
Population: 5,400,000

SLOVENIA
Capital: Ljubljana
Area: 20,251 sq km (7,819 sq miles)
Population: 2,000,000

YUGOSLAVIA
Capital: Belgrade
Area: 102,173 sq km (39,449 sq miles)
Population: 10,600,00

MAP QUIZ

✦ The goddess Athena gave her name to the Greek capital. What is it?

✦ On which island are the Ruins of Knossos?

✦ The walled town of Dubrovnik looks over which sea?

✦ Where can you see a Roman Amphitheatre?

✦ In which city is the Cathedral of St Vitus?

✦ Can you find a mountain range in Romania?

✦ The capital of Slovakia has its own castle. What is its name?

✦ Where are Skoda cars made?

✦ Name a monastery in Bulgaria.

NORTHERN EURASIA

THIS REGION SPANS two continents, Europe and Asia, separated by the Ural Mountains. Asia is bigger than Europe, taking up about 75 per cent of the land area, but only about 35 per cent of the people live there.

In the east lies Siberia, much of which is uninhabited wilderness. The climate there is extremely cold, and in winter the temperature falls below -45°C (-49°F), but this area is rich in gems and oil.

From 1922 to 1991, northern Eurasia was one vast country, called the Union of Soviet Socialist Republics, or USSR. The world's largest country, it was made up of 15 republics, each with a communist government. In 1991, the USSR split apart and all the republics became independent. The largest – the Russian Federation – remained dominant and drew many of the new nations into a Commonwealth of Independent States.

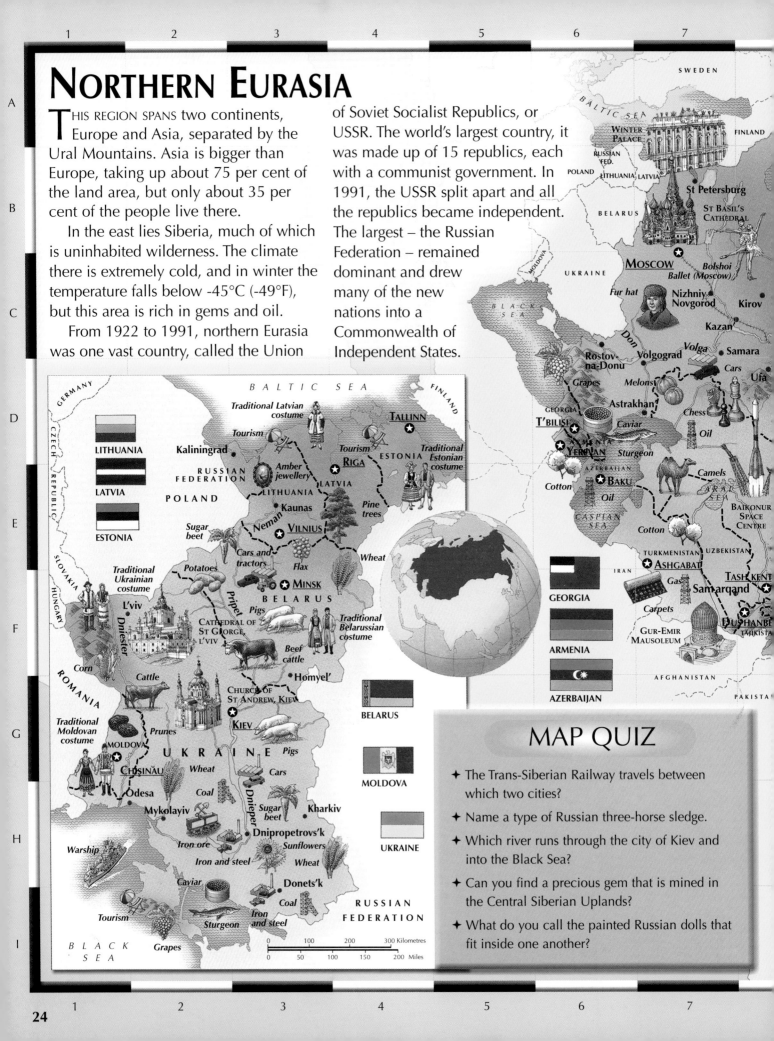

SWEDEN
BALTIC SEA
WINTER PALACE
FINLAND
RUSSIAN FED.
POLAND
LITHUANIA LATVIA
St Petersburg
ST BASIL'S CATHEDRAL
BELARUS
MOLDOVA
UKRAINE
MOSCOW
Bolshoi Ballet (Moscow)
Fur hat
Nizhniy Novgorod
Kirov
BLACK SEA
Kazan
Don
Volgograd
Volga
Samara
Rostov-na-Donu
Grapes
Melons
Cars
Ufa
GEORGIA
Astrakhan
Chess
Oil
T'BILISI
Caviar
ARMENIA
YEREVAN
Sturgeon
Camels
Cotton
AZERBAIJAN
BAKU
Oil
ARAL SEA
CASPIAN SEA
BAIKONUR SPACE CENTRE
Cotton
TURKMENISTAN
UZBEKISTAN
IRAN
ASHGABAT
TASHKENT
Gas
Samarqand
GEORGIA
Carpets
GUR-EMIR MAUSOLEUM
DUSHANBE
TAJIKISTAN
ARMENIA
AFGHANISTAN
AZERBAIJAN
PAKISTAN

GERMANY
BALTIC SEA
FINLAND
Traditional Latvian costume
Tourism
TALLINN
LITHUANIA
Kaliningrad
RUSSIAN FEDERATION
Tourism
RIGA
ESTONIA
Traditional Estonian costume
CZECH REPUBLIC
LATVIA
POLAND
Amber jewellery
LITHUANIA
LATVIA
ESTONIA
Sugar beet
Kaunas
Neman
Pine trees
SLOVAKIA
Traditional Ukrainian costume
Potatoes
Cars and tractors
VILNIUS
Flax
Wheat
HUNGARY
L'viv
CATHEDRAL OF ST GEORGE, L'VIV
MINSK
Pripet
BELARUS
Pigs
Traditional Belarussian costume
Corn
Dniester
Cattle
Beef cattle
Homyel'
ROMANIA
Traditional Moldovan costume
Prunes
CHURCH OF ST ANDREW, KIEV
KIEV
Pigs
MOLDOVA
UKRAINE
Pigs
CHIŞINĂU
Wheat
Cars
Odesa
Coal
Dnieper
Sugar beet
Kharkiv
Mykolayiv
Dnipropetrovs'k
Iron ore
Sunflowers
Wheat
Iron and steel
Warship
Caviar
Donets'k
Coal
RUSSIAN FEDERATION
Tourism
Sturgeon
Iron and steel
BLACK SEA
Grapes

BELARUS
MOLDOVA
UKRAINE

0   100   200   300 Kilometres
0 50 100 150 200 Miles

MAP QUIZ

✦ The Trans-Siberian Railway travels between which two cities?

✦ Name a type of Russian three-horse sledge.

✦ Which river runs through the city of Kiev and into the Black Sea?

✦ Can you find a precious gem that is mined in the Central Siberian Uplands?

✦ What do you call the painted Russian dolls that fit inside one another?

FACTS AND FIGURES

Largest lake:
Caspian Sea (the largest lake in the world) covers an area of 3,600,000 sq km (143,205 sq miles).

World's longest railway:
Trans-Siberian, Moscow to Nakhodka near Vladivostok, 9,438 km (5,864 miles).

ARMENIA
Capital: Yerevan
Area: 29,800 sq km (11,490 sq miles)
Population: 3,500,000
Languages: Armenian, Russian

AZERBAIJAN
Capital: Baku
Area: 86,600 sq km (33,340 sq miles)
Population: 7,700,000
Language: Azerbaijani

BELARUS
Capital: Minsk
Area: 207,600 sq km (80,134 sq miles)
Population: 10,300,000
Languages: Belarussian, Russian

ESTONIA
Capital: Tallinn
Area: 45,100 sq km (17,413 sq miles)
Population: 1,400,000
Language: Estonian

GEORGIA
Capital: T'bilisi
Area: 69,700 sq km (26,900 sq miles)
Population: 5,000,000
Language: Georgian

KAZAKHSTAN
Capital: Astana
Area: 2,717,300 sq km (1,049,155 sq miles)
Population: 16,200,000
Languages: Kazakh, Russian

KYRGYZSTAN
Capital: Bishkek
Area: 198,500 sq km (76,640 sq miles)
Population: 4,700,000
Languages: Kyrgyz, Russian

LATVIA
Capital: Riga
Area: 63,700 sq km (24,595 sq miles)
Population: 2,400,000
Languages: Latvian, Russian

LITHUANIA
Capital: Vilnius
Area: 65,200 sq km (25,170 sq miles)
Population: 3,700,000
Language: Lithuanian

MOLDOVA
Capital: Chisinau
Area: 33,700 sq km (13,000 sq miles)
Population: 4,400,000
Languages: Romanian, Moldovan

RUSSIAN FEDERATION
Capital: Moscow
Area: 17,075,000 sq km (6,592,637 sq miles)
Population: 147,000,000
Language: Russian

TAJIKISTAN
Capital: Dushanbe
Area: 143,100 sq km (55,240 sq miles)
Population: 6,200,000
Languages: Tajik, Russian

TURKMENISTAN
Capital: Ashgabat
Area: 488,100 sq km (188,455 sq miles)
Population: 4,500,000
Languages: Turkmen, Russian

UKRAINE
Capital: Kiev
Area: 603,700 sq km (231,990 sq miles)
Population: 50,700,000
Languages: Ukrainian, Russian

UZBEKISTAN
Capital: Tashkent
Area: 447,400 sq km (172,741 sq miles)
Population: 24,300,000
Languages: Uzbek, Russian

UNITED STATES AND CANADA

THE COUNTRIES THAT FORM North America are two of the largest and richest in the world; Canada is second only to the Russian Federation in land area, yet it has only about one tenth the population of the United States, its smaller neighbour. Canada has ten provinces and three territories, while the United States is made of up 50 states plus the District of Columbia (D.C.) where Washington, the capital, is located.

The original inhabitants of North America were once called 'Indians'; Canadian tribes are now more correctly known as 'First Nation' people, and those of the U.S. as 'Native Americans'. Similarly, the term 'Eskimo', previously used for natives of the far north, has been replaced by 'Inuit'. Today, the population of both countries is a mix of racial backgrounds: European, African, Asian, and Hispanic (Spanish speaking) from Central and South America.

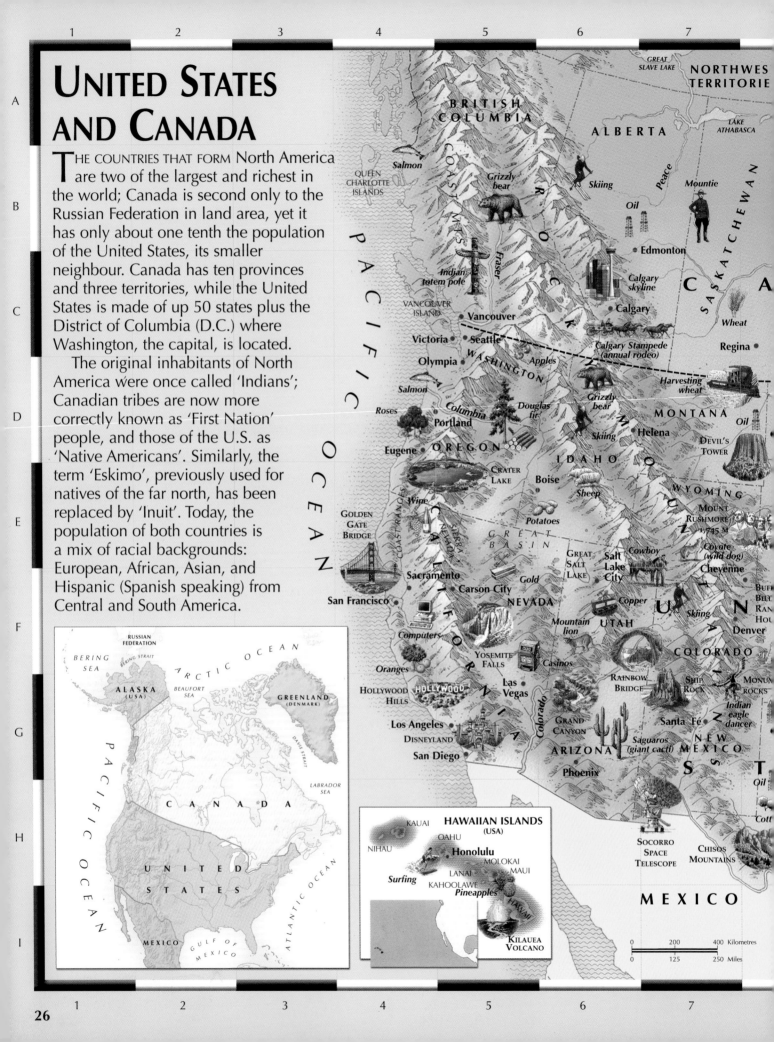

GREAT SLAVE LAKE
NORTHWEST TERRITORIE
BRITISH COLUMBIA
ALBERTA
LAKE ATHABASCA
Salmon
Grizzly bear
Skiing
Peace
Mountie
Oil
Edmonton
Calgary skyline
SASKATCHEWAN
C A
Indian totem pole
Fraser
Calgary
QUEEN CHARLOTTE ISLANDS
VANCOUVER ISLAND
Vancouver
Victoria
Seattle
Olympia
WASHINGTON
Apples
Calgary Stampede (annual rodeo)
Wheat
Regina
Harvesting wheat
Salmon
Columbia
Portland
Douglas fir
Grizzly bear
MONTANA
Oil
Roses
Eugene
OREGON
Skiing
Helena
DEVIL'S TOWER
CRATER LAKE
Boise
IDAHO
Wine
SIERRA NEVADA
Potatoes
Sheep
WYOMING
MOUNT RUSHMORE 1,745 M
GOLDEN GATE BRIDGE
COAST RANGES
GREAT BASIN
GREAT SALT LAKE
Cowboy
Coyote (wild dog)
Cheyenne
Sacramento
Gold
Salt Lake City
Copper
Carson City
NEVADA
UTAH
Skiing
Denver
BUFF BILL RAN HOU
Computers
Mountain lion
COLORADO
Oranges
YOSEMITE FALLS
Casinos
RAINBOW BRIDGE
SHIP ROCK
MONU ROCKS
HOLLYWOOD HILLS
HOLLYWOOD
Las Vegas
Colorado
GRAND CANYON
Santa Fé
Indian eagle dancer
Los Angeles
DISNEYLAND
Saguaros (giant cacti)
NEW MEXICO
San Diego
ARIZONA
S T
Phoenix
Oil
SOCORRO SPACE TELESCOPE
CHISOS MOUNTAINS
Cott
CALIFORNIA
PACIFIC OCEAN
MEXICO

RUSSIAN FEDERATION
BERING SEA
BERING STRAIT
ARCTIC OCEAN
ALASKA (USA)
BEAUFORT SEA
GREENLAND (DENMARK)
DAVIS STRAIT
LABRADOR SEA
C A N A D A
PACIFIC OCEAN
U N I T E D S T A T E S
ATLANTIC OCEAN
MEXICO
GULF OF MEXICO

HAWAIIAN ISLANDS (USA)
KAUAI
OAHU
NIHAU
Honolulu
MOLOKAI
LANAI
MAUI
Surfing
KAHOOLAWE
Pineapples
HAWAII
KILAUEA VOLCANO

0   200   400 Kilometres
0   125   250 Miles

FACTS AND FIGURES

UNITED STATES OF AMERICA
Capital: Washington, DC
Area: 9,166,600 sq km (3,539,224 sq miles)
Population: 278,400,000
Language: English
Religion: Christian
Currency: US dollar
Government: Multiparty Republic

CANADA
Capital: Ottawa
Area: 9,976,139 sq km (3,851,817 sq miles)
Population: 31,282,000
Language: English, French
Religion: Christian
Currency: Canadian dollar
Government: Parliamentary democracy

MEXICO AND CENTRAL AMERICA

CENTRAL AMERICA IS a land bridge joining the continents of North and South America. At its narrowest point, in Panama, a canal 82 km (51 miles) long links the Atlantic and Pacific oceans. There are seven countries in Central America. To the north lies Mexico and to the east lie the islands of the Caribbean, which are often called the West Indies. In the Caribbean, local poverty and tourist luxury exist side by side.

During the 16th century, the islands were settled by Europeans, who shipped black slaves from Africa to work on the farms. Today the population is a mixture of many peoples. The main languages are English, Spanish, and dialects called patois: mixtures of African languages with French or English.

There are great contrasts in the area's climate and vegetation, from the Mexican desert in the north to the southern rainforests and the coral islands in the east. Sometimes tropical storms called hurricanes rage through the Caribbean, their high winds and huge waves causing devastating damage.

Map labels

Tijuana
Mexicali
Cotton
Cotton
Gila monster
Copper
Ciudad Juárez
Saguaro cactus
Hermosillo
Armadillo
Elephant seal
Cattle
Chihuahua
Pack donkey
Rattlesnake
MEXICO
Rio Grande
Rice
Silver
Grey whales
MEXICO
Boojum tree
Gold
Torreón
Monterrey
Sardines
Saltillo
Iron and steel
Brown pelicans
Monarch butterfly
Folk dancers
Anchovies
Tuna
Citrus fruit
Flamingos
Shrimps
Huichol Indian
Oil
Lobster
Grapes
CHICHÉN ITZÁ (MAYA CITY)
Tourism
Tourism
Aguascalientes
Tampico
León
NATIONAL CATHEDRAL (MEXICO CITY)
Shrimps
Guadalajara
Scarlet macaw
Tequila
MEXICO CITY
Puebla
Veracruz
Oil
Oil
TIKAL (MAYA CITY)
Beliz City
Swordfish
POPOCATÉPETL VOLCANO 5,452 m
Tzeltal Indian
BEL
Fisherman on Lake Pátzcuaro
OLMEC HEAD
BELMOP
Tourism
Acapulco
GUATEMALA
Aztec god
GUATEMALA CITY
Quetzal
Coffee
Banana
Shrimps
SAN SALVADOR
Cott
PACIFIC OCEAN
GULF OF CALIFORNIA
GULF OF MEXICO
U S A

MEXICO

MAP QUIZ

- ✦ In what country would you find a gila monster?

- ✦ Which Caribbean islands are famous for steel bands?

- ✦ Name the volcano that lies close to Mexico City.

- ✦ Where would you go to buy world-famous cigars?

- ✦ In what country is the ancient Mayan city of Tikal?

- ✦ In which island country was reggae music born?

GUATEMALA
BELIZE
HONDURAS
EL SALVADOR

EL SALVADOR
NICARAGUA
COSTA RICA
PANAMA

ATLANTIC OCEAN

U S A

FACTS AND FIGURES

Jamaica ("island of springs") is a popular tourist resort.

CUBA
Capital: Havana

DOMINICA
Capital: Roseau

DOMINICAN REPUBLIC
Capital: Santo Domingo

EL SALVADOR
Capital: San Salvador

GRENADA
Capital: St George's

GUADELOUPE
Capital: Basse Terre

GUATEMALA
Capital: Guatemala City

HAITI
Capital: Port-au-Prince

HONDURAS
Capital: Tegucigalpa

JAMAICA
Capital: Kingston

MARTINIQUE
Capital: Fort-de-France

MEXICO
Capital: Mexico City

NETHERLANDS ANTILLES
Capital: Willemstad

NICARAGUA
Capital: Managua

PANAMA
Capital: Panama City

PUERTO RICO
Capital: San Juan

ST KITTS & NEVIS
Capital: Basseterre

ST LUCIA
Capital: Castries

ST VINCENT & THE GRENADINES
Capital: Kingstown

TRINIDAD & TOBAGO
Capital: Port-of-Spain

ANTIGUA & BARBUDA
Capital: St John's

ARUBA
Capital: Oranjestad

BAHAMAS
Capital: Nassau

BARBADOS
Capital: Bridgetown

BELIZE
Capital: Belmopan

COSTA RICA
Capital: San José

DOMINICA

ST LUCIA

ST KITTS & NEVIS

ANTIGUA & BARBUDA

BAHAMAS

ST VINCENT & THE GRENADINES

BARBADOS

GRENADA

TRINIDAD & TOBAGO

CUBA

JAMAICA

HAITI

DOMINICAN REPUBLIC

Tourism

B A H A M A S

NASSAU

Cruise liner

Scuba diver

STRAITS OF FLORIDA

Sugar cane

Coral reefs

Pineapples

HAVANA

C U B A

Cigars

Scuba diver

CAYMAN ISLANDS (UK)

JAMAICA

Reggae music

Rum

Kingston

Green turtle

Grapefruit

Coffee

TURKS & CAICOS ISLANDS (UK)

Coffee

HAITI

Port-au-Prince

DOMINICAN REPUBLIC

Santo Domingo

Cocoa

Sharks

Coral reefs

Tourism

SAN JUAN

PUERTO RICO (US)

VIRGIN ISLANDS (USA/UK)

Sailing

Frigate bird

ANGUILLA (UK)

ST KITTS & NEVIS

MONTSERRAT (UK)

ANTIGUA & BARBUDA

GUADELOUPE (Fr)

Coconuts

DOMINICA

MARTINIQUE (Fr)

ST LUCIA

BARBADOS

ST VINCENT & THE GRENADINES

C A R I B B E A N   S E A

Nutmeg and mace

GRENADA

Steel bands

TRINIDAD & TOBAGO

HONDURAS

Cattle

TEGUCIGALPA

Coffee

Bananas

NICARAGUA

MANAGUA

Coffee

San José

COSTA RICA

Toucan

PANAMA CANAL

P A N A M A

PANAMA CITY

Spider monkey

COLOMBIA

ARUBA (Neth)

NETHERLANDS ANTILLES (Neth)

V E N E Z U E L A

0   200   400   600   800 Kilometres
0   100   200   300   400   500 Miles

SOUTH AMERICA

THE CONTINENT of South America is dominated by the snow-capped Andes mountains and the wide Amazon river, which flows through the vast rainforests of the north. South of the Amazon are the grassy plains of the Pampas and vast expanses of barren, windswept desert. South America's wealth comes from agriculture, tourism and the export of beef. Natural resources such as coal, copper, gold, iron ore, lead, natural gas, oil and tin also contribute.

During the 16th century, the land was settled by Europeans, who conquered many of the native peoples. Among these were the Incas, whose civilization flourished in the Peruvian Andes until it was destroyed in 1532-33 by Spanish conquistadors.

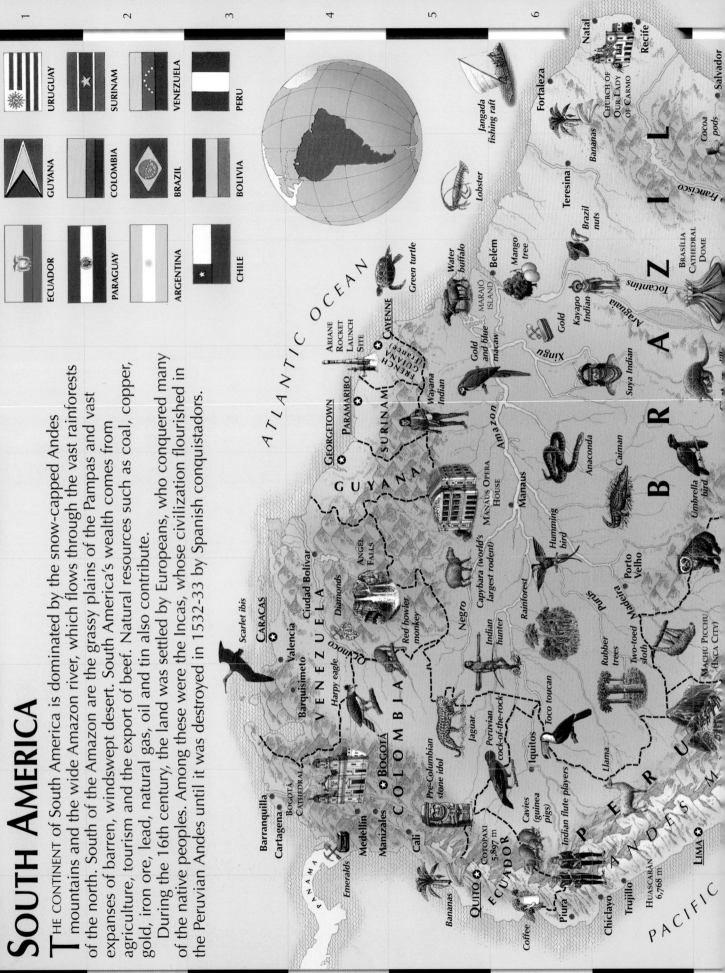

URUGUAY
SURINAM
VENEZUELA
PERU
GUYANA
COLOMBIA
BRAZIL
BOLIVIA
ECUADOR
PARAGUAY
ARGENTINA
CHILE

ATLANTIC OCEAN

PACIFIC

Natal
Recife
CHURCH OF OUR LADY OF CARMO
Salvador
Cocoa pods
Fortaleza
Bananas
Jangada fishing raft
Teresina
Brazil nuts
Lobster
Water buffalo
Belém
Mango tree
MARAJÓ ISLAND
BRASÍLIA CATHEDRAL DOME
Gold
Kayapo Indian
Tocantins
Araguaia
Xingu
Gold and blue macaw
Suya Indian
ARIANE ROCKET LAUNCH SITE
CAYENNE
FRENCH GUIANA (France)
Green turtle
Wayana Indian
PARAMARIBO
GEORGETOWN
SURINAM
Amazon
Anaconda
Caiman
GUYANA
MANAUS OPERA HOUSE
Manaus
Humming bird
Umbrella bird
B R A Z I L
Rainforest
Porto Velho
Madeira
Two-toed sloth
Rubber trees
Purus
Capybara (world's largest rodent)
Indian hunter
Negro
MACHU PICCHU (INCA CITY)
Scarlet ibis
CARACAS
Valencia
Ciudad Bolívar
Diamonds
ANGEL FALLS
Barquisimeto
Red howler monkey
Harpy eagle
VENEZUELA
Toco toucan
Iquitos
Llama
Jaguar
Peruvian cock-of-the-rock
Barranquilla
Cartagena
BOGOTÁ CATHEDRAL
BOGOTÁ
Medellín
Manizales
Cali
COLOMBIA
Pre-Columbian stone idol
Cavies (guinea pigs)
Indian flute players
PANAMA
Emeralds
QUITO
ECUADOR
COTOPAXI 5,897 m
Bananas
Coffee
Piura
Chiclayo
Trujillo
HUASCARÁN 6,768 m
ANDES MTS
P E R U
LIMA
Orinoco

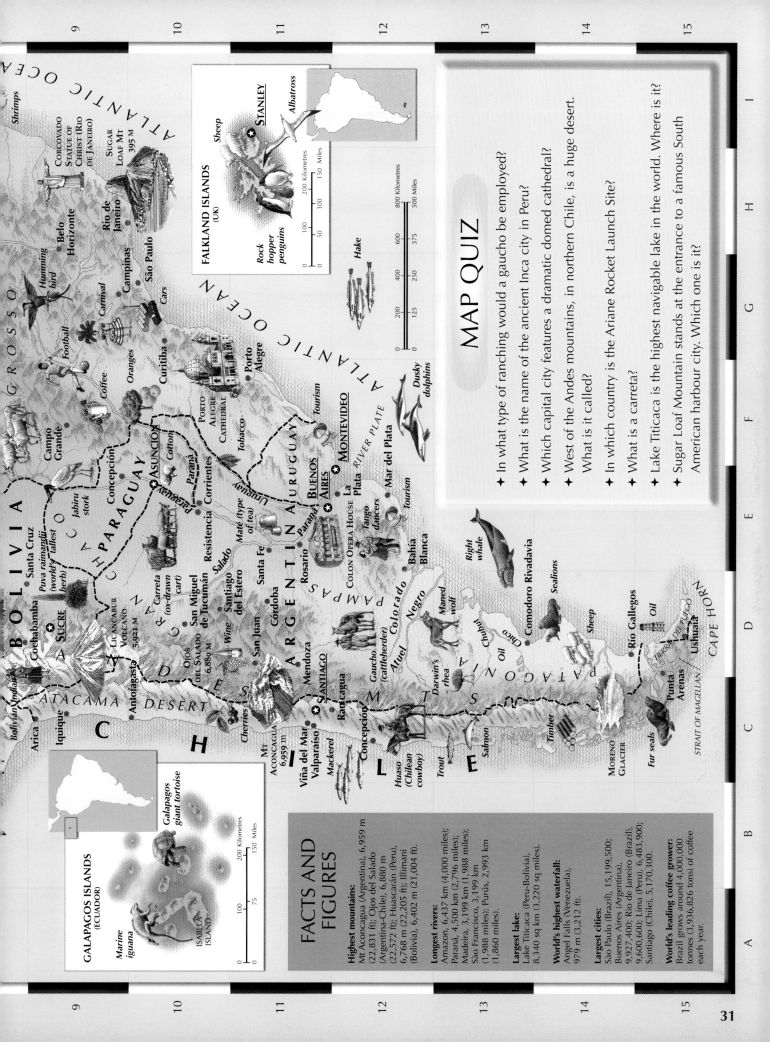

ATLANTIC OCEAN

Shrimps

CORCOVADO STATUE OF CHRIST (RIO DE JANEIRO)

SUGAR LOAF MT 395 M

Humming bird

Belo Horizonte

Rio de Janeiro

Carnival

Campinas

São Paulo

Football

Coffee

Oranges

Cars

Curitiba

Porto Alegre

PORTO ALEGRE CATHEDRAL

Tobacco

Coffee

Campo Grande

MATO GROSSO

Puya raimondii (world's tallest herb)

Jabiru stork

Cotton

Concepción

ASUNCIÓN

Paraná

PARAGUAY

Paraguay

CHACO

Corrientes

Resistencia

Maté (type of tea)

Uruguay

Salado

URUGUAY

MONTEVIDEO

Tourism

Dusky dolphins

Santa Cruz

Cochabamba

BOLIVIA

SUCRE

Bolivian Indians

Arica

Iquique

ATACAMA DESERT

Antofagasta

LICANCABUR VOLCANO 5,921 M

OJOS DEL SALADO 6,880 M

ANDES

San Miguel de Tucumán

Santiago del Estero

Santa Fe

Córdoba

Rosario

Paraná

La Plata

BUENOS AIRES

RIVER PLATE

Mar del Plata

Tourism

COLON OPERA HOUSE

Tango dancers

Wine

San Juan

ARGENTINA

PAMPAS

Mendoza

SANTIAGO

Rancagua

Mt ACONCAGUA 6,959 M

Cherries

Viña del Mar

Valparaíso

Concepción

CHILE

Mackerel

Salmon

Trout

Huaso (Chilean cowboy)

Gaucho (cattleherder)

Colorado

Atuel

Negro

Maned wolf

Darwin's rhea

PATAGONIA

Chubut

Oil

Chico

Comodoro Rivadavia

Sealions

Right whale

Sheep

Timber

Fur seals

MORENO GLACIER

Río Gallegos

Oil

Punta Arenas

TIERRA DEL FUEGO

Ushuaia

STRAIT OF MAGELLAN

CAPE HORN

FALKLAND ISLANDS (UK)

Sheep

STANLEY

Albatross

Rock hopper penguins

Hake

200 Kilometres
150 Miles
100
50

800 Kilometres
500 Miles
600
375
400
250
200
125

ATLANTIC OCEAN

GALAPAGOS ISLANDS (ECUADOR)

Marine iguana

Galapagos giant tortoise

ISABELA ISLAND

200 Kilometres
150 Miles
100
75

MAP QUIZ

- In what type of ranching would a gaucho be employed?
- What is the name of the ancient Inca city in Peru?
- Which capital city features a dramatic domed cathedral?
- West of the Andes mountains, in northern Chile, is a huge desert. What is it called?
- In which country is the Ariane Rocket Launch Site?
- What is a carreta?
- Lake Titicaca is the highest navigable lake in the world. Where is it?
- Sugar Loaf Mountain stands at the entrance to a famous South American harbour city. Which one is it?

FACTS AND FIGURES

Highest mountains:
Mt Aconcagua (Argentina), 6,959 m (22,831 ft); Ojos del Salado (Argentina-Chile), 6,880 m (22,572 ft); Huascarán (Peru), 6,768 m (22,205 ft); Illimani (Bolivia), 6,402 m (21,004 ft).

Longest rivers:
Amazon, 6,437 km (4,000 miles); Paraná, 4,500 km (2,796 miles); Madeira, 3,199 km (1,988 miles); São Francisco, 3,199 km (1,988 miles); Purús, 2,993 km (1,860 miles).

Largest lake:
Lake Titicaca (Peru-Bolivia), 8,340 sq km (3,220 sq miles).

World's highest waterfall:
Angel Falls (Venezuela), 979 m (3,212 ft).

Largest cities:
São Paulo (Brazil), 15,199,500; Buenos Aires (Argentina), 9,927,400; Rio de Janeiro (Brazil), 9,600,600; Lima (Peru), 6,483,900; Santiago (Chile), 5,170,300.

World's leading coffee grower:
Brazil grows around 4,000,000 tonnes (3,936,826 tons) of coffee each year.

THE MIDDLE EAST

THE MIDDLE EAST (also known as southwest Asia) lies at the join of three continents – Asia, Africa, and Europe – and takes in many different landscapes. There is a wide variety too, in cultures and religions, and these differences have resulted in longstanding political instability in the region.

The countries surrounding the Mediterranean are wetter than the others, and crops such as citrus fruits, olives and wheat are grown there. To the south stretch the huge deserts of Saudi Arabia. Earlier this century, the world's largest deposits of oil were discovered in the countries around the Gulf, and the oil-fields in the region now supply the world.

Some of the world's first settled farming communities grew up in the Fertile Crescent, which stretches from the Mediterranean to the area between the Tigris and Euphrates rivers. Of great historical interest, too, is the city of Jerusalem, which is a holy place for Christians, Muslims and Jews, visited by millions of people each year.

MAP QUIZ

- ✦ An old Syrian city gives its name to a luxurious textile weave. What is it?

- ✦ The ancient city of Baghdad lies on what river?

- ✦ Which sea is known for its caviar-producing sturgeon?

- ✦ What is a traditional Arab sailing boat called?

- ✦ From which tree does the biblical perfume called Frankincense come?

- ✦ A country in this region has the same name as its capital city. Which one is it?

- ✦ What mountain range borders the Gulf in Iran?

- ✦ On which sea does the city of Jedda lie?

- ✦ Can you find two textile fibres that are produced in the Middle East?

- ✦ Muslim women cover their faces in public. What is the name of the veil they wear?

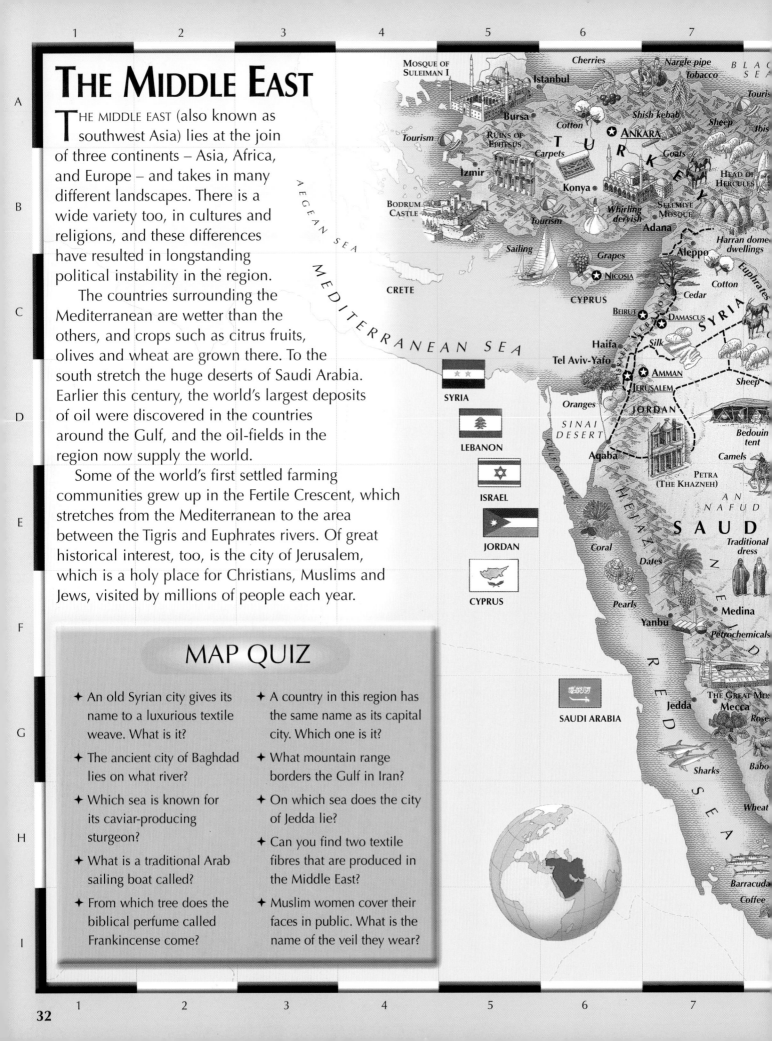

SYRIA

LEBANON

ISRAEL

JORDAN

CYPRUS

SAUDI ARABIA

FACTS AND FIGURES

Dhow (Arab boat) off the Yemen coast.

Largest city:
Tehran (Iran), 8,712,100.

Hottest capital:
Riyadh, Saudi Arabia, is the hottest capital city in the world, with average July temperatures of over 40°C (104°F).

Dunes are formed when desert winds blow the sand into mounds.

BAHRAIN
Capital: Manama
Area: 678 sq km (262 sq miles)

CYPRUS
Capital: Nicosia
Area: 9,251 sq km (3,571 sq miles)

IRAN
Capital: Tehran
Area: 1,648,000 sq km (636,297 sq miles)

IRAQ
Capital: Baghdad
Area: 438,317 sq km (169,235 sq miles)

ISRAEL
Capital: Jerusalem
Area: 20,770 sq km (8,017 sq miles) plus the Golan Heights and West Bank, total area 7,418 sq km (2,864 sq miles)

JORDAN
Capital: Amman
Area: 89,206 sq km (34,443 sq miles)

KUWAIT
Capital: Kuwait
Area: 17,818 sq km (6,879 sq miles)

LEBANON
Capital: Beirut
Area: 10,400 sq km (4,015 sq miles)

OMAN
Capital: Muscat
Area: 212,457 sq km (82,030 sq miles)

QATAR
Capital: Doha
Area: 11,000 sq km (4,247 sq miles)

SAUDI ARABIA
Capital: Riyadh
Area: 2,149,690 sq km (830,001 sq miles)

SYRIA
Capital: Damascus
Area: 185,180 sq km (71,500 sq miles)

TURKEY
Capital: Ankara
Area: 779,452 sq km (300,948 sq miles)

UNITED ARAB EMIRATES
Capital: Abu Dhabi
Area: 83,600 sq km (32,278 sq miles)

YEMEN
Capital: Sana
Area: 527,968 sq km (203,850 sq miles)

SOUTHERN ASIA

THE LARGEST COUNTRY in Southern Asia is India, and the region is often called the "Indian subcontinent". Over one billion people live there – about 22 per cent of the world's population. Most people live in the fertile river and coastal plains. Nearly three-quarters are farmers, who depend heavily on seasonal rains. The most important crop is rice.

India was united in the 16th and 17th centuries under Mogul rule. In the 18th century, it became part of the British Empire, but gained independence in 1947, when it was divided into two: Hindu India and Muslim Pakistan. In 1971, east Pakistan became a separate country, Bangladesh.

Today, Pakistan and India are industrial nations. Pakistan's industries include food processing, textiles and chemicals. India produces oil, coal, manganese, iron ore, and copper, and has iron and steel, car manufacturing, and computer industries.

Scale bar:
0 — 200 — 400 — 600 — 800 Kilometres
0 — 100 — 200 — 300 — 400 — 500 Miles

MAP QUIZ

+ Hindu people believe the Ganges River is holy. In which mountain range is its source?

+ Through what countries does the region's longest river, the Indus, flow?

+ Where could you see 'giraffe-necked' women with metal rings around their throat?

+ In which city is the huge Victoria Railway Terminus?

+ Name the traditional Indian loincloth woven from undyed, homespun cotton.

+ Can you locate the highest mountain in Southern Asia?

+ What island is famous for its thriving trade in tea?

+ Which stringed instrument, sometimes used in western music, is associated with India?

+ What two countries are linked by the Kyber Pass?

+ Where would you go to find both ruby and jade mines?

+ In Burma (Myanmar), which animal is used to haul heavy teak logs?

Map labels

TURKMENISTAN
UZBEKISTAN
TAJIKISTAN
Veiled Afghan women
Carpets
HINDU KUSH
K2 (MT GODWIN AUSTEN) 8,611 m
Lapis lazuli
KHYBER PASS
Herat
KABUL
Snow leopard
AFGHANISTAN
ISLAMABAD
Afghan headgear
Peaches
RHOTAS FORT
Lahore
GOLDEN TEMPLE (AMRITSAR)
Sikh
Bactrian camel
PAKISTAN
JAMIA MOSQUE (QUETTA)
BADSHAHI MOSQUE
PARLIAMENT HOUSE
Camels
Delhi
NEW DELHI
TOMB OF MUHAMMAD ALI JINNAH
Cotton
Indus
THAR DESERT
Agra
Jaipur
Hyderabad
Wheat
PALACE OF THE WINDS
Millet
Sari
Chemicals
Karachi
AFGHANISTAN (flag)
Green turtle
Sheep and goats
Peanuts
INDIA
Cars
PAKISTAN (flag)
Dhow (Arab boat)
VICTORIA RAILWAY TERMINUS (BOMBAY)
Iron Cotton and steel
Cattle
Mumbai (Bombay)
Pune
Cotton
ARABIAN SEA
Sitar player
Hyderabad
Indian cobra
Pepper
Herrings
Temple elephant
Coconut palms
Bangalore
Prawns
INDIA (flag)
MEENAKSHI TEMPLE
Sardines

Mountain Peaks in the Himalayas

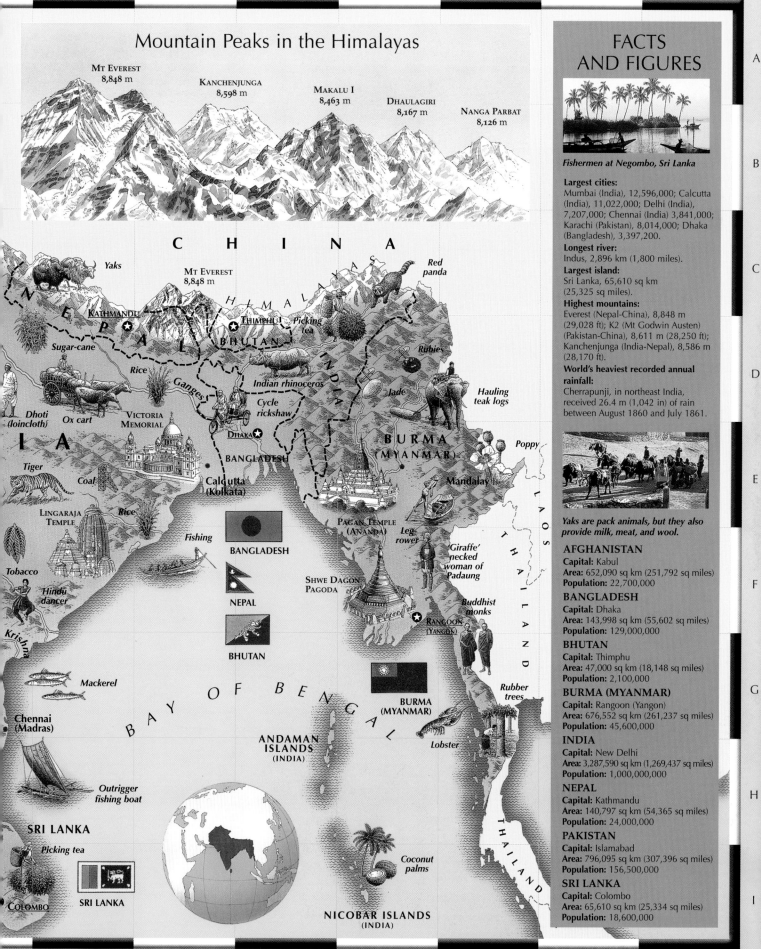

MT EVEREST 8,848 m

KANCHENJUNGA 8,598 m

MAKALU I 8,463 m

DHAULAGIRI 8,167 m

NANGA PARBAT 8,126 m

C H I N A

Yaks

MT EVEREST 8,848 m

Red panda

H I M A L A Y A S

KATHMANDU

THIMPHU

Picking tea

Sugar-cane

N E P A L

BHUTAN

Rubies

Rice

Ganges

Indian rhinoceros

Jade

Hauling teak logs

Cycle rickshaw

I N D I A

Dhoti (loincloth)

Ox cart

VICTORIA MEMORIAL

DHAKA

BURMA (MYANMAR)

Poppy

I A

BANGLADESH

Tiger

Coal

Calcutta (Kolkata)

Mandalay

LINGARAJA TEMPLE

Rice

Fishing

PAGAN TEMPLE (ANANDA)

Leg rower

Giraffe' necked woman of Padaung

BANGLADESH

Tobacco

Hindu dancer

NEPAL

SHWE DAGON PAGODA

Buddhist monks

Krishna

BHUTAN

RANGOON (YANGON)

Mackerel

L A O S

T H A I L A N D

Rubber trees

Chennai (Madras)

B A Y   O F   B E N G A L

BURMA (MYANMAR)

Lobster

ANDAMAN ISLANDS (INDIA)

Outrigger fishing boat

SRI LANKA

Picking tea

THAILAND

Coconut palms

SRI LANKA

COLOMBO

NICOBAR ISLANDS (INDIA)

FACTS AND FIGURES

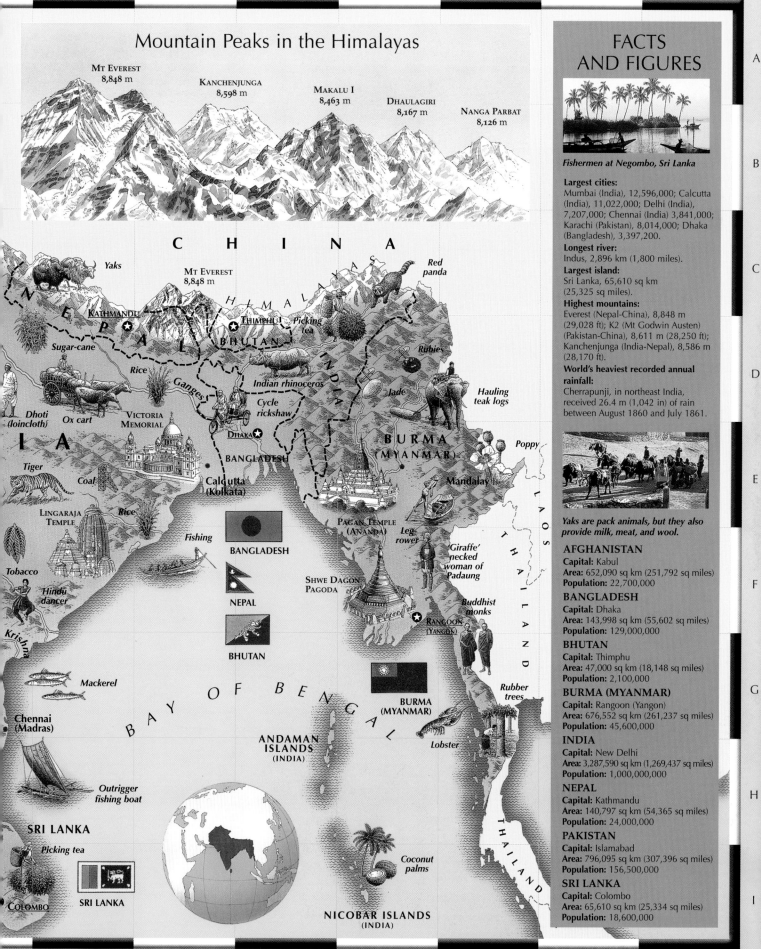

Fishermen at Negombo, Sri Lanka

Largest cities:
Mumbai (India), 12,596,000; Calcutta (India), 11,022,000; Delhi (India), 7,207,000; Chennai (India) 3,841,000; Karachi (Pakistan), 8,014,000; Dhaka (Bangladesh), 3,397,200.

Longest river:
Indus, 2,896 km (1,800 miles).

Largest island:
Sri Lanka, 65,610 sq km (25,325 sq miles).

Highest mountains:
Everest (Nepal-China), 8,848 m (29,028 ft); K2 (Mt Godwin Austen) (Pakistan-China), 8,611 m (28,250 ft); Kanchenjunga (India-Nepal), 8,586 m (28,170 ft).

World's heaviest recorded annual rainfall:
Cherrapunji, in northeast India, received 26.4 m (1,042 in) of rain between August 1860 and July 1861.

Yaks are pack animals, but they also provide milk, meat, and wool.

AFGHANISTAN
Capital: Kabul
Area: 652,090 sq km (251,792 sq miles)
Population: 22,700,000

BANGLADESH
Capital: Dhaka
Area: 143,998 sq km (55,602 sq miles)
Population: 129,000,000

BHUTAN
Capital: Thimphu
Area: 47,000 sq km (18,148 sq miles)
Population: 2,100,000

BURMA (MYANMAR)
Capital: Rangoon (Yangon)
Area: 676,552 sq km (261,237 sq miles)
Population: 45,600,000

INDIA
Capital: New Delhi
Area: 3,287,590 sq km (1,269,437 sq miles)
Population: 1,000,000,000

NEPAL
Capital: Kathmandu
Area: 140,797 sq km (54,365 sq miles)
Population: 24,000,000

PAKISTAN
Capital: Islamabad
Area: 796,095 sq km (307,396 sq miles)
Population: 156,500,000

SRI LANKA
Capital: Colombo
Area: 65,610 sq km (25,334 sq miles)
Population: 18,600,000

JAPAN

LYING EAST OF THE MAIN PART OF ASIA, Japan is made up of four major islands – Hokkaido, Honshu, Shikoku, and Kyushu – and thousands of smaller ones. In this area, where two plates of the Earth's crust meet, earthquakes are common.

Nearly three-quarters of the country is mountainous and wooded, but the areas that are suitable for agriculture are cultivated very efficiently. The main crop is rice. Because so little of the land can be farmed, the Japanese eat a lot of fish, and they catch more fish than any other nation. Most of Japan's 126 million people live on a small area of flat, largely coastal, land, mainly around the great south-coast cities of Honshu island, such as Nagoya, Tokyo and Osaka.

In the last 40 years Japan has become one of the world's most important industrial nations. This is all the more remarkable because the oil and most of the raw materials that are needed in manufacturing have to be imported. Japanese cars, electrical goods, ships, cameras, and many other products are exported all over the world.

MAP QUIZ

- ✦ Mount Fuji, Japan's highest mountain, is located on which of the four main islands?
- ✦ For more than 1,000 years, the city of Kyoto was the capital of Japan. Where is Kyoto?
- ✦ Which style of formal wrestling originated in Japan?
- ✦ An important religious shrine is shown on Honshu island. What faith does it represent?
- ✦ What kind of food is tofu?

- ✦ Can you find the location of an annual snow festival?
- ✦ Name a type of theatre that is popular in Japan.
- ✦ Which gem is found in the seas around Japan?
- ✦ What is the name of the ancient fortified castle on the Japanese island of Shikoku?
- ✦ Miniature trees are highly prized in Japanese culture. What are they called?

KURIL ISLANDS (RUSS. FED.)

Nemuro
Japanese crane
Trout
Kushiro
Pollock
Steller's sea eagle
Ceremonial Ainu dress
Teshio
HOKKAIDO
Brown bear
Coal
Potatoes
Timber
Paper
Fish owl
Cod
Sapporo
Snow festival
Muroran
MT YOTEI 1,893 m
JAPAN
Hakodate
TAPPI-ZAKI
Fukushima
Halibut
Fishing boats
Saury
Mackerel
Oysters
Crab
SEA OF JAPAN
Anchovies
Aomori
Apples
Sake
Akita
Bonsai (miniature trees)
Judo
Japanese arts
Morioka
Sendai
Rice planting
Fish flags (carp streamers)
Sardines
Fukushima
Automatic rice planter
Coal
SADO
HONSHU
PACIFIC OCEAN

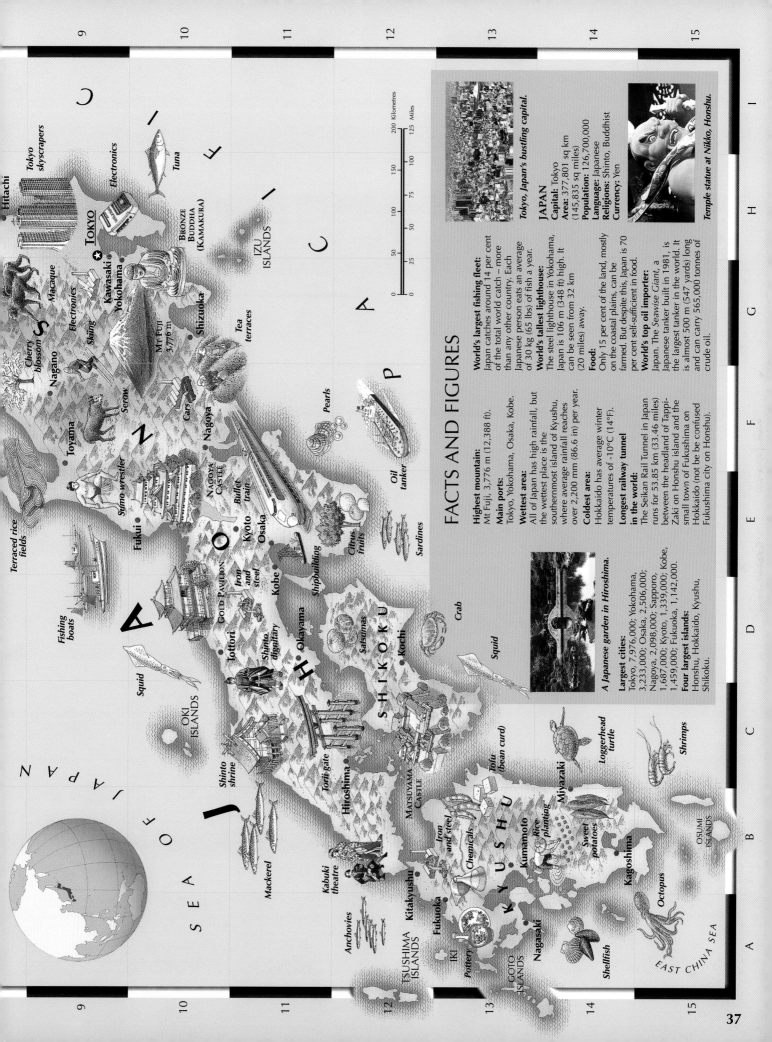

FACTS AND FIGURES

Highest mountain:
Mt Fuji, 3,776 m (12,388 ft).

Main ports:
Tokyo, Yokohama, Osaka, Kobe.

Wettest area:
All of Japan has high rainfall, but the wettest place is the southernmost island of Kyushu, where average rainfall reaches over 2,200 mm (86.6 in) per year.

Coldest area:
Hokkaido has average winter temperatures of -10°C (14°F).

Longest railway tunnel in the world:
The Seikan Rail Tunnel in Japan runs for 53.85 km (33.46 miles) between the headland of Tappi-Zaki on Honshu Island and the small town of Fukushima on Hokkaido (not be confused with Fukushima city on Honshu).

Largest cities:
Tokyo, 7,976,000; Yokohama, 3,233,000; Osaka, 2,506,000; Nagoya, 2,098,000; Sapporo, 1,687,000; Kyoto, 1,339,000; Kobe, 1,459,000; Fukuoka, 1,142,000.

Four largest islands:
Honshu, Hokkaido, Kyushu, Shikoku.

World's largest fishing fleet:
Japan catches around 14 per cent of the total world catch – more than any other country. Each Japanese person eats an average of 30 kg (65 lbs) of fish a year.

World's tallest lighthouse:
The steel lighthouse in Yokohama, Japan is 106 m (348 ft) high. It can be seen from 32 km (20 miles) away.

Food:
Only 15 per cent of the land, mostly on the coastal plains, can be farmed. But despite this, Japan is 70 per cent self-sufficient in food.

World's top oil importer:
Japan. The Seawise Giant, a Japanese tanker built in 1981, is the largest tanker in the world. It is almost 500 m (547 yards) long and can carry 565,000 tonnes of crude oil.

Tokyo, Japan's bustling capital.

JAPAN
Capital: Tokyo
Area: 377,801 sq km (145,835 sq miles)
Population: 126,700,000
Language: Japanese
Religions: Shinto, Buddhist
Currency: Yen

Temple statue at Nikko, Honshu.

A Japanese garden in Hiroshima.

JAPAN

SEA OF JAPAN

EAST CHINA SEA

PACIFIC OCEAN

HONSHU
SHIKOKU
KYUSHU

Hitachi
Tokyo skyscrapers
Electronics
Tuna
TOKYO
Kawasaki
Yokohama
Electronics
BRONZE BUDDHA (KAMAKURA)
Shizuoka
IZU ISLANDS
Macaque
Cherry blossom
Nagano
Skiing
Serow
Mt Fuji 3,776 m
Tea terraces
Toyama
Sumo wrestler
Fukui
Cars
Nagoya
NAGOYA CASTLE
Bullet train
Kyoto
Osaka
Pearls
Iron and steel
Kobe
GOLD PAVILION
Shipbuilding
Citrus fruits
Oil tanker
Sardines
Terraced rice fields
Fishing boats
OKI ISLANDS
Squid
Tottori
Shinto dignitary
Okayama
Satsumas
Crab
Squid
Toriï gate
Hiroshima
MATSUYAMA CASTLE
Shinto shrine
SHIKOKU
Kochi
Loggerhead turtle
Shrimps
Mackerel
Kabuki theatre
Kitakyushu
Fukuoka
IKI
Pottery
TSUSHIMA ISLANDS
Anchovies
GOTO ISLANDS
Nagasaki
Shellfish
KYUSHU
Kumamoto
Iron and steel
Chemicals
Rice planting
Tofu (bean curd)
Miyazaki
Sweet potatoes
Kagoshima
Octopus
OSUMI ISLANDS

200 Kilometres
125 Miles
0 25 50 75 100 150

37

SOUTHEASTERN ASIA

SOUTHEASTERN ASIA is a strip of mainland and thousands of islands. Indonesia, with the fifth largest population in the world, consists of more than 13,000 islands. The Philippines is a collection of over 7,000 islands. To the east is the tiny country of Brunei, whose Sultan (ruler) is said to be the world's richest person.

The climate in this region is hot and wet, with heavy seasonal rains. Thick forests cover much of it, though many trees have been cleared for timber and for agriculture.

From the 16th to the 19th century, the region was colonized by Europeans, but during the 20th century, all the countries regained their independence.

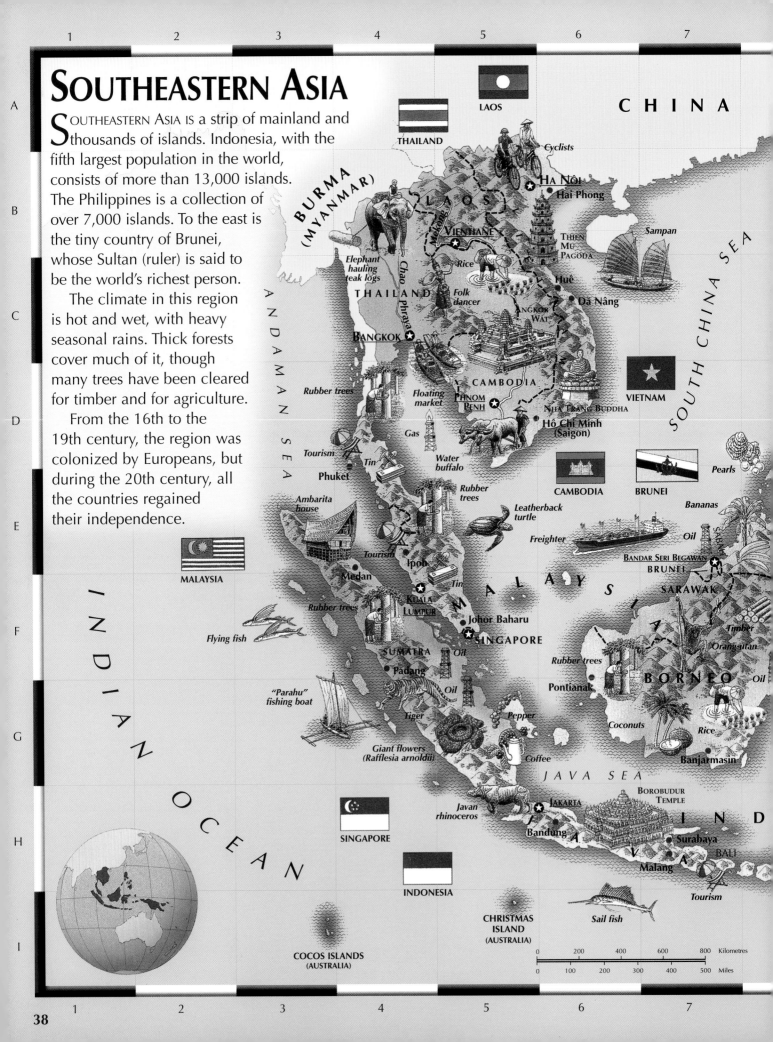

CHINA

LAOS

THAILAND

BURMA (MYANMAR)

Cyclists

HA NỘI

Hai Phong

Elephant hauling teak logs

Chao Phraya

LAOS

VIENTIANE

THIEN MU PAGODA

Sampan

Rice

Huế

SOUTH CHINA SEA

Folk dancer

Đà Nẵng

ANGKOR WÁT

THAILAND

BANGKOK

CAMBODIA

Rubber trees

Floating market

PHNOM PENH

NHA TRANG BUDDHA

VIETNAM

Gas

Hồ Chí Minh (Saigon)

Tourism

Water buffalo

Phuket

Tin

CAMBODIA

BRUNEI

Pearls

Rubber trees

Leatherback turtle

Bananas

Ambarita house

Freighter

Oil

Tourism

Ipoh

SABAH

Medan

Tin

BANDAR SERI BEGAWAN

BRUNEI

MALAYSIA

Rubber trees

KUALA LUMPUR

MALAYSIA

SARAWAK

Johor Baharu

Timber

SINGAPORE

Orang-utan

Flying fish

SUMATRA

Oil

Rubber trees

BORNEO

Oil

Padang

Pontianak

"Parahu" fishing boat

Oil

Coconuts

Rice

INDIAN OCEAN

Tiger

Pepper

Coffee

Banjarmasin

Giant flowers (Rafflesia arnoldii)

JAVA SEA

BOROBUDUR TEMPLE

Javan rhinoceros

JAKARTA

SINGAPORE

Bandung

JAVA

Surabaya

BALI

INDONESIA

Malang

Tourism

CHRISTMAS ISLAND (AUSTRALIA)

Sail fish

COCOS ISLANDS (AUSTRALIA)

	0	200	400	600	800	Kilometres
	0	100	200	300	400	500	Miles

FACTS AND FIGURES

Largest cities:
Jakarta (Indonesia), 9,000,000;
Manila (Philippines), 7,729,000;
Bangkok (Thailand), 5,875,900;
Ho Chi-Minh (Vietnam,
previously called Saigon),
4,075,700.

Highest mountain:
Puncak Jaya (Indonesia),
5,040 m (16,503 ft).

Largest island:
New Guinea, 808,510 sq km
(312,168 sq miles).

Longest river:
Mekong, 4,184 km
(2,600 miles).

Longest name in the world:
The Thai name for Bangkok
is Krungthep maha nakorn,
amarn rattanakosindra,
mahindrayudhya, mahadilok
pop noparatana rajdhani
mahasathan, amorn piman
avatarn satit, sakkatultiya
visanukarn prasit.

BRUNEI
Capital: Bandar Seri Begawan
Area: 5,765 sq km (2,225 sq miles)
Population: 328,000
Languages: Malay, English
Religions: Muslim, Buddhist

CAMBODIA
Capital: Phnom Pénh
Area: 181,035 sq km
(69,881 sq miles)
Population: 11,200,000
Languages: Khmer
Religion: Buddhist

INDONESIA
Capital: Jakarta
Area: 1,904,569 sq km
(735,412 sq miles)
Population: 212,000,000
Language: Indonesian
Religion: Muslim

LAOS
Capital: Vientiane
Area: 236,800 sq km (91,435 sq miles)

Population: 5,400,000
Language: Lao
Religion: Buddhist

MALAYSIA
Capital: Kuala Lumpur
Area: 329,749 sq km
(127,326 sq miles)
Population: 22,200,000
Languages: Malay, English, Chinese
Religions: Muslim, Buddhist

PAPUA NEW GUINEA
Capital: Port Moresby
Area: 462,840 sq km
(178,716 sq miles)
Population: 4,800,000
Languages: English, numerous
others
Religion: Christian

PHILIPPINES
Capital: Manila
Area: 300,000 sq km
(115,839 sq miles)
Population: 76,000,000

Languages: Filipino, English,
Spanish
Religion: Christian

SINGAPORE
Capital: Singapore
Area: 618 sq km (239 sq miles)
Population: 3,600,000
Languages: Malay, Chinese, English
Religion: Taoist, Buddhist

THAILAND
Capital: Bangkok
Area: 513,115 sq km
(198,129 sq miles)
Population: 61,400,000
Language: Thai
Religion: Buddhist

VIETNAM
Capital: Ha Nôi
Area: 329,558 sq km
(127,252 sq miles)
Population: 79,800,000
Languages: Vietnamese, Chinese
Religion: Buddhist

MAP QUIZ

+ Perahu fishing boats sail along the coast of which country?

+ Offshore oil is responsible for the fabulous wealth of which tiny Southeast Asian nation?

+ The Mekong River runs through two countries on the map. Can you name them?

+ What sea lies off Vietnam?

+ Where is the Buddhist temple of Angkor Wat?

TAIWAN

Rice terraces

MANILA
LUZON

PHILIPPINES

PHILIPPINES

Sugar cane

Cebu

Monkey-eating eagle

Coral reefs

MINDANAO

Zamboanga

Davao

PACIFIC OCEAN

Vinta boat

Coral reefs

CELEBES SEA

Coconuts

Sago palms

Sago palms

Tuna

MOLUCCAS

Oil

Oil

Jayapura

Spirit house

Coconuts

Toraja house

Shrimps

Nutmeg

CERAM SEA

CERAM

IRIAN JAYA

NEW GUINEA

NEW BRITAIN

CELEBES

Cloves

Crabs

Tree kangaroo

PUNCAK JAYA 5,040 m

Mt Wilhelm 4,500 m

PAPUA NEW GUINEA

Coffee

BANDA SEA

Irian Jaya native

Dancer and drum

Ujungpandang

INDONESIA

Komodo dragon

Maize

DILI

Asmat warriors

Bird of paradise

PORT MORESBY

FLORES

PART OF EAST TIMOR

TIMOR

EAST TIMOR

ARAFURA SEA

PAPUA NEW GUINEA

SUMBA

Kupang

TIMOR SEA

AUSTRALIA

CHINA AND NORTHEASTERN ASIA

MORE PEOPLE LIVE in China than in any other country. China has over one billion inhabitants, so one person in every five in the world is Chinese. China is also the world's third largest country, after the Russian Federation and Canada. Most people live in the east of China, where the climate is wet and the land is fertile. In most places the farms are owned by each village, so everyone works on them and shares the harvest.

Tibet lies in the highlands of southwest China at an average height of 4,500 m (14,800 ft) above sea level. This is higher than most mountains in Europe and the United States. The Himalayas, the world's highest mountains, stretch along the border between China and India.

After a long civil war in China, a communist government was formed in 1949 by Mao Zedong. The defeated nationalists set up a rival Republic of China on the island of Taiwan, which is still independent. The province of Hong Kong, once a British colony, became part of China in 1997. In Korea, a war was fought in the 1950s between communist and non-communist forces. Korea is now divided into two countries, North Korea and South Korea.

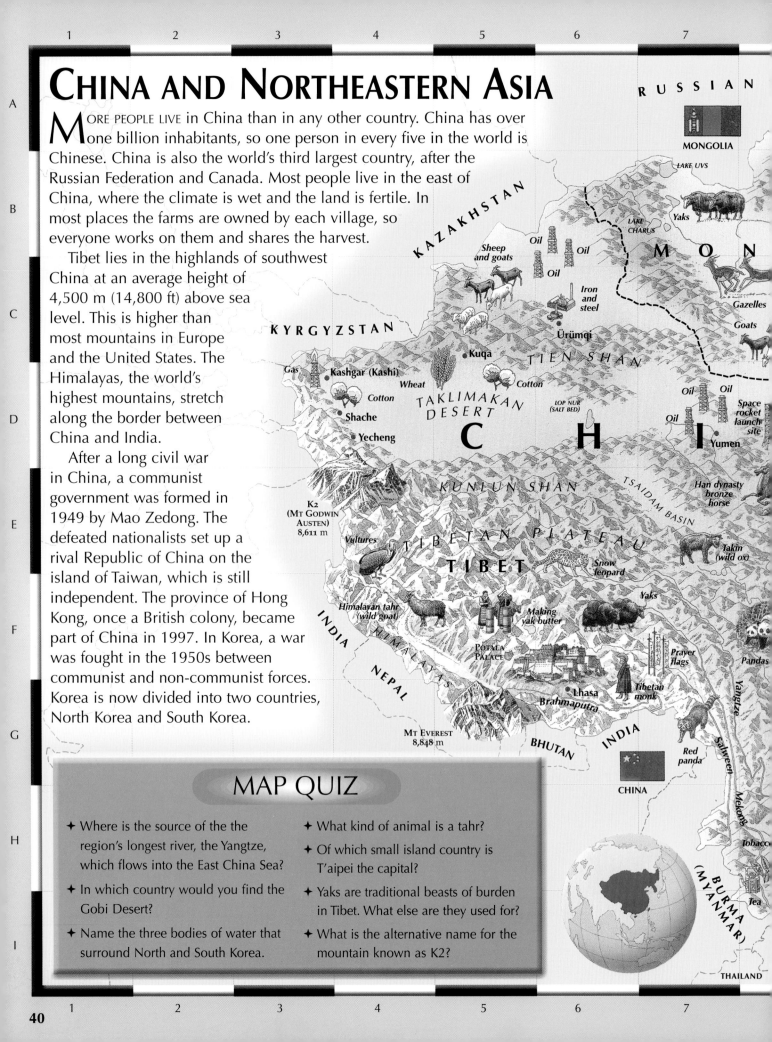

RUSSIAN

MONGOLIA

LAKE UVS

KAZAKHSTAN

Yaks

LAKE CHARUS

M O N

Oil

Sheep and goats

Oil

Oil

Oil

Gazelles

Iron and steel

Goats

Ürümqi

KYRGYZSTAN

Kuqa

TIEN SHAN

Gas

Kashgar (Kashi)

Wheat

Cotton

TAKLIMAKAN DESERT

Cotton

LOP NUR (SALT BED)

Oil

Oil

Space rocket launch site

Shache

C H I

Oil

Yecheng

Yumen

KUNLUN SHAN

TSAIDAM BASIN

Han dynasty bronze horse

K2 (MT GODWIN AUSTEN) 8,611 m

Vultures

TIBETAN PLATEAU

Takin (wild ox)

TIBET

Snow leopard

Yaks

Himalayan tahr (wild goat)

Making yak butter

INDIA

HIMALAYAS

POTALA PALACE

Prayer flags

Pandas

NEPAL

Lhasa

Tibetan monk

Brahmaputra

Yangtze

MT EVEREST 8,848 m

BHUTAN

INDIA

Red panda

Salween

Mekong

CHINA

Tobacco

BURMA (MYANMAR)

Tea

THAILAND

MAP QUIZ

+ Where is the source of the the region's longest river, the Yangtze, which flows into the East China Sea?

+ In which country would you find the Gobi Desert?

+ Name the three bodies of water that surround North and South Korea.

+ What kind of animal is a tahr?

+ Of which small island country is T'aipei the capital?

+ Yaks are traditional beasts of burden in Tibet. What else are they used for?

+ What is the alternative name for the mountain known as K2?

FACTS AND FIGURES

The Great Wall of China, built to protect the northern border, is nearly 3,460 km (2,150 miles) long.

Longest river:
Yangtze (Chang Jiang), 6,300 km (3,915 miles).

Largest city:
Shanghai (China), 13,510,000.

The gateway to the Chaotain Palace in the historic city of Nanjing, formerly China's capital.

CHINA
Capital: Beijing (Peking)
Area: 9,598,055 sq km (3,704,863 sq miles)
Population: 1,300,000,000
Language: Chinese
Religions: Confucianist, Buddhist, Taoist, Muslim
Currency: Yuan
Government: Communist republic

MONGOLIA
Capital: Ulan Bator
Area: 1,565,000 sq km (604,247 sq miles)
Population: 2,700,000
Language: Mongolian
Religions: Buddhist, Lamaist, Muslim
Currency: Tugrik
Government: Republic

NORTH KOREA
Capital: P'yongyang
Area: 120,538 sq km (46,540 sq miles)
Population: 24,000,000
Language: Korean
Religions: Buddhist, Confucianist, Taoist
Currency: North Korean Won
Government: Communist republic

SOUTH KOREA
Capital: Seoul
Area: 99,016 sq km (38,230 sq miles)
Population: 46,800,000
Language: Korean
Religions: Buddhist, Confucianist, Christian
Currency: South Korean Won
Government: Multiparty Republic

TAIWAN
Capital: T'aipei
Area: 35,990 sq km (13,890 sq miles)
Population: 22,000,000
Language: Chinese
Religions: Buddhist, Taoist, Christian
Currency: Taiwan dollar
Government: Multiparty Republic

AFRICA

A FLAT PLATEAU broken by mountain ranges, Africa stretches about 4,000 km (2,500 miles) north and south of the equator. Dominating north Africa are the Mediterranean coastline and the Sahara Desert; to the south are the grasslands of east Africa, the rainforest of the Zaire basin and the farmlands of Kenya, Uganda and Tanzania.

Some African countries have agricultural economies: maize, coffee, tea, fruit, tobacco and cotton are typical crops. Others are rich in gold, diamonds, oil, copper and iron. Many regions, though, are desperately poor, and their people suffer constantly from disease and famine.

MAP QUIZ

◆ The highest peak in Africa is Mt Kilimanjaro. Where is it!

◆ In what country can you see the pyramids at Giza, which were built as tombs for ancient rulers?

◆ Can you name the world's longest river, which flows through Africa into the Mediterranean Sea?

◆ The largest desert on earth is also on this continent. What is it called?

◆ What is a felucca?

◆ Which country has three capital cities?

MEDITERRANEAN SEA

ATLANTIC OCEAN

RED SEA

Olives

Wine

TUNIS

TUNISIA

Benghazi

Citrus fruits

Dates

Oil

LIBYA

Alexandria

Pyramids at Giza

Port Said

Suez Canal

CAIRO

EGYPT

GREAT TEMPLE AT ABU SIMBEL

LAKE NASSER

Nile

Felucca (Egyptian boat)

Port Sudan

PYRAMIDS AT MEROE

NUBIAN DESERT

KHARTOUM

Blue Nile

White Nile

SUDAN

Nile crocodile

Striped hyena

Nuba tribesmen

Coffee

ASMARA

ERITREA

Ras Dashen 4,620 M

ADDIS ABABA

ETHIOPIA

Great white pelican

Lions

Giraffes

Oryx

Nomadic tribesman

DJIBOUTI

GULF OF ADEN

Dhow (Arab boat)

MALIA

Cheetah

Elephant

CENTRAL AFRICAN REPUBLIC

CHAD

NDJAMENA

LAKE CHAD

Chari Hippopotami

Ogone

ROON

Tibesti Massif

Nomadic caravan

Jerboa

SAHARA

Scorpion

Horned viper

ROMAN COLOSSEUM AT EL-JEM

ALGIERS

ALGERIA

HOGGAR MTS

TRIPOLI

Tangier

STRAIT OF GIBRALTAR

RABAT

Casablanca

Marrakech

Citrus fruits

MOROCCO

ATLAS MTS

Tanning leather

Mt. TOUBKAL 4,165 M

Tuareg horseman

Iron ore

Sardines

LAÂYOUNE

WESTERN SAHARA (occupied by Morocco)

NOUAKCHOTT

MAURITANIA

Camels

DAKAR

SENEGAL

BANJUL

Bissau

GUINEA BISSAU

GUINEA

CONAKRY

SIERRA LEONE

FREETOWN

MONROVIA

LIBERIA

Diamonds

IVORY COAST

YAMOUSSOUKRO

Abidjan

Gold

GHANA

Bananas

BURKINA

OUAGADOUGOU

Grain store

Sheep

Goats

iron ore

BAMAKO

MALI

Timbuktu

JENNE MOSQUE

Niger

NIAMEY

NIGER

Ostriches

Wodaabe herdsman

Nigerian women

Tuareg noble

Bedouin tent

Donkey with water skin

Emir's guard

Kano

KANO MOSQUE

NIGERIA

Niger

Lagos

ABUJA

Groundnuts

BENIN

TOGO

Nigerian women

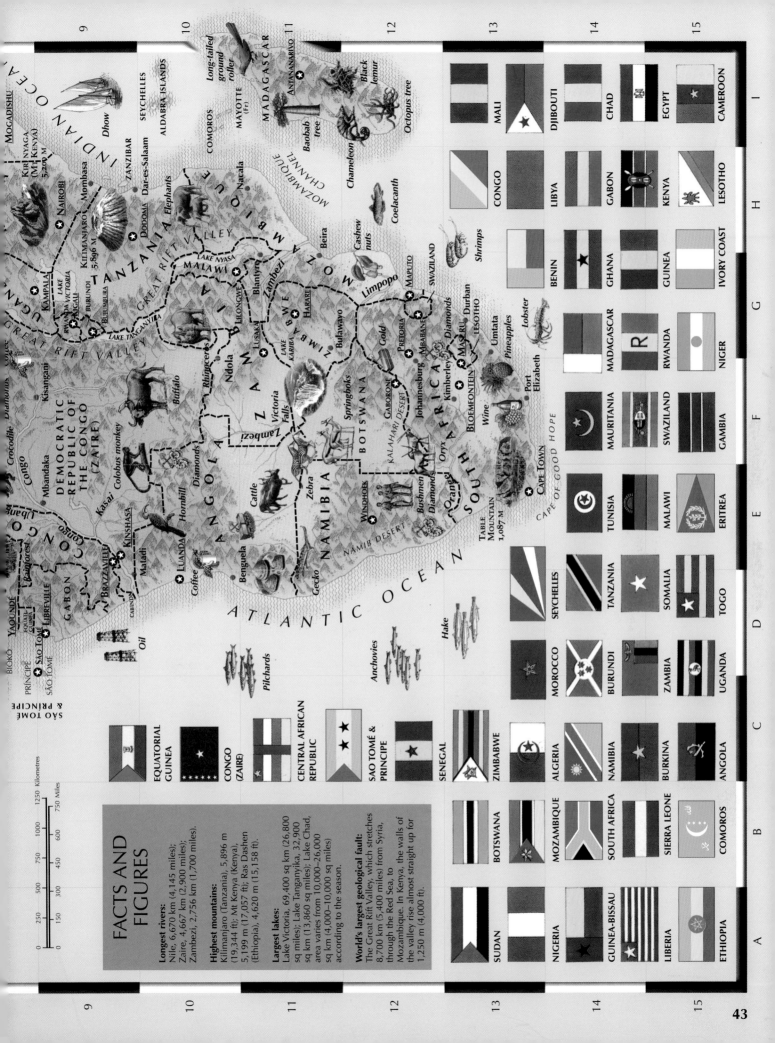

FACTS AND FIGURES

Longest rivers:
Nile, 6,670 km (4,145 miles); Zaire, 4,667 km (2,900 miles); Zambezi, 2,756 km (1,700 miles).

Highest mountains:
Kilimanjaro (Tanzania), 5,896 m (19,344 ft); Mt Kenya (Kenya), 5,199 m (17,057 ft); Ras Dashen (Ethiopia), 4,620 m (15,158 ft).

Largest lakes:
Lake Victoria, 69,400 sq km (26,800 sq miles); Lake Tanganyika, 32,900 sq km (13,860 sq miles); Lake Chad, area varies from 10,000–26,000 sq km (4,000–10,000 sq miles) according to the season.

World's largest geological fault:
The Great Rift Valley, which stretches 8,700 km (5,400 miles) from Syria, through the Red Sea, to Mozambique. In Kenya, the walls of the valley rise almost straight up for 1,250 m (4,000 ft).

Kilometres: 0 250 500 750 1000 1250
Miles: 0 150 300 450 600 750

Flags

MALI, DJIBOUTI, CHAD, EGYPT, CAMEROON, CONGO, LIBYA, GABON, KENYA, LESOTHO, BENIN, GHANA, GUINEA, IVORY COAST, MADAGASCAR, RWANDA, NIGER, MAURITANIA, SWAZILAND, GAMBIA, TUNISIA, MALAWI, ERITREA, SEYCHELLES, TANZANIA, SOMALIA, TOGO, MOROCCO, BURUNDI, ZAMBIA, UGANDA, EQUATORIAL GUINEA, CONGO (ZAIRE), CENTRAL AFRICAN REPUBLIC, SAO TOMÉ & PRINCIPE, SENEGAL, ZIMBABWE, ALGERIA, NAMIBIA, BURKINA, ANGOLA, BOTSWANA, MOZAMBIQUE, SOUTH AFRICA, SIERRA LEONE, COMOROS, SUDAN, NIGERIA, GUINEA-BISSAU, LIBERIA, ETHIOPIA

Map labels

INDIAN OCEAN, ATLANTIC OCEAN, MADAGASCAR, MOZAMBIQUE CHANNEL, GREAT RIFT VALLEY, TANZANIA, MALAWI, ZAMBIA, ZIMBABWE, MOZAMBIQUE, BOTSWANA, NAMIBIA, ANGOLA, DEMOCRATIC REPUBLIC OF THE CONGO (ZAIRE), GABON, CONGO, UGANDA, SOUTH AFRICA, SWAZILAND, LESOTHO

MOGADISHU, KIRINYAGA (MT KENYA) 5,200 M, NAIROBI, Mombasa, KILIMANJARO 5,896 M, ZANZIBAR, Dar-es-Salaam, DODOMA, KAMPALA, LAKE VICTORIA, KIGALI, RWANDA, BURUNDI, BUJUMBURA, Lake Tanganyika, Kisangani, Mbandaka, KINSHASA, Matadi, BRAZZAVILLE, LIBREVILLE, YAOUNDÉ, MALABO, BIOKO, SÃO TOMÉ, PRÍNCIPE, SÃO TOMÉ & PRÍNCIPE, LUANDA, Benguela, Cabinda, WINDHOEK, NAMIB DESERT, KALAHARI DESERT, GABORONE, PRETORIA, Johannesburg, Kimberley, BLOEMFONTEIN, MASERU, MBABANE, MAPUTO, Durban, Port Elizabeth, CAPE TOWN, CAPE OF GOOD HOPE, TABLE MOUNTAIN 1,087 M, Bulawayo, HARARE, LAKE KARIBA, Ndola, Lusaka, LILONGWE, Blantyre, LAKE NYASA, Beira, Nacala, COMOROS, MAYOTTE (Fr), ANTANANARIVO, ALDABRA ISLANDS, SEYCHELLES

SÃO TOMÉ & PRÍNCIPE, LAKE VICTORIA, Zambezi, Limpopo, Orange, Kasai, Congo, Ubangi, Bangoui, Kwango

Dhow, Long-tailed ground roller, Black lemur, Baobab tree, Chameleon, Octopus tree, Coelacanth, Shrimps, Cashew nuts, Lobster, Pineapples, Diamonds, Wine, Springboks, Oryx, Bushmen, Diamonds, Gold, Gecko, Zebra, Cattle, Buffalo, Rhinoceros, Colobus monkey, Hornbill, Crocodile, Diamonds, Oil, Coffee, Pilchards, Anchovies, Hake, Elephants, Victoria Falls, Rainforest

AUSTRALIA

AUSTRALIA IS A country and a continent. Much of it is hot and dry, especially in the sparsely populated central deserts. Most people live where the climate is wetter, east of the Great Dividing Range and on the island of Tasmania. Two-thirds of all Australians live in cities, particularly Sydney, Melbourne, and Brisbane. The population of Australia is only 17.9 million people, compared with 278 million in the United States.

Millions of years ago, Australia drifted away from the other continents, so many plants and animals that evolved there are not found anywhere else. Some mammals, such as kangaroos, are marsupials: they rear their young in pouches on their stomachs.

The first inhabitants appeared about 100,000 years ago and Aboriginal Australians are their descendants. Europeans did not arrive until 200 years ago. Since 1945 the population has doubled, with people coming to Australia from many parts of the world.

MAP QUIZ

✦ Uluru (Ayers Rock) is near which group of mountains?

✦ Name the two coastal cities joined by the Indian-Pacific Railway.

✦ Where would you find an international opera house whose design was inspired by sailing ships?

✦ The Port Arthur Penal Settlement is located on which island?

✦ What is the common name for an Australian wild dog?

✦ Which remote town provides a base for the flying doctor service?

✦ Can you find the place where a meteorite landed in Australia?

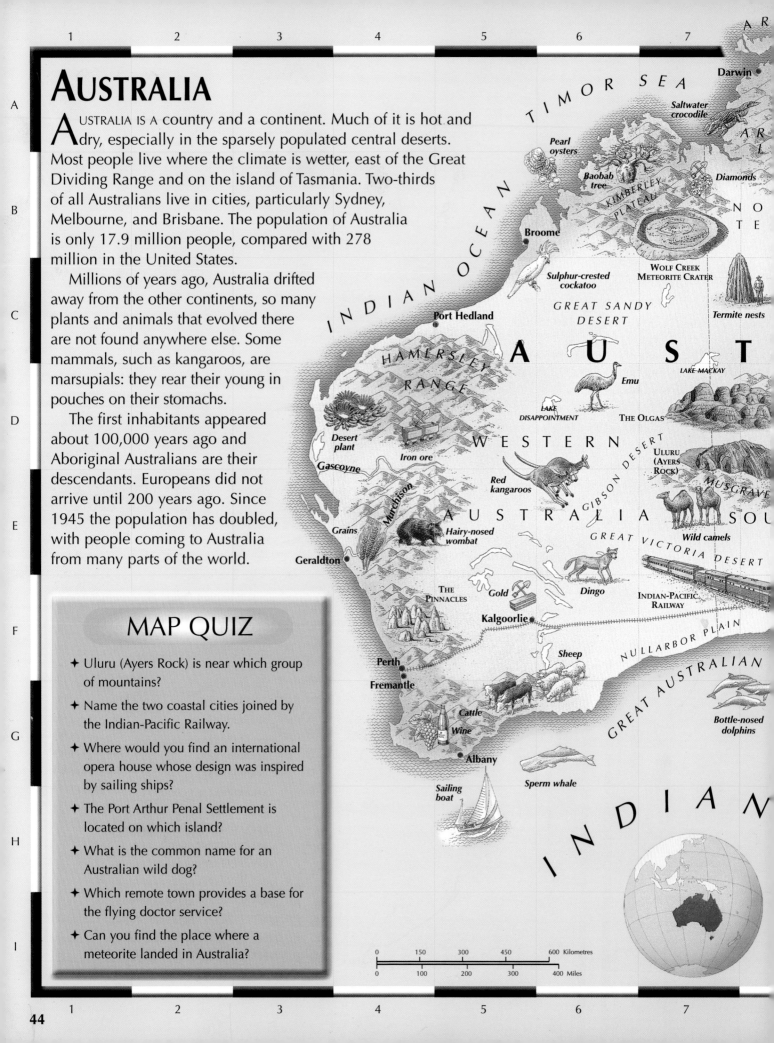

TIMOR SEA

Darwin

Saltwater crocodile

A R L

ARNHEM

N O T E

Pearl oysters

Baobab tree

KIMBERLEY PLATEAU

Diamonds

Broome

INDIAN OCEAN

Sulphur-crested cockatoo

WOLF CREEK METEORITE CRATER

GREAT SANDY DESERT

Termite nests

Port Hedland

A U S T

HAMERSLEY RANGE

Emu

LAKE MACKAY

LAKE DISAPPOINTMENT

THE OLGAS

Desert plant

WESTERN

Iron ore

ULURU (AYERS ROCK)

Gascoyne

Red kangaroos

GIBSON DESERT

MUSGRAVE

Murchison

A U S T R A L I A

S O U

Grains

Hairy-nosed wombat

GREAT VICTORIA DESERT

Wild camels

Geraldton

Dingo

INDIAN-PACIFIC RAILWAY

THE PINNACLES

Gold

Kalgoorlie

NULLARBOR PLAIN

Perth

Sheep

GREAT AUSTRALIAN

Fremantle

Bottle-nosed dolphins

Cattle

Wine

Albany

Sailing boat

Sperm whale

INDIAN

| 0 | 150 | 300 | 450 | 600 Kilometres |
| 0 | 100 | 200 | 300 | 400 Miles |

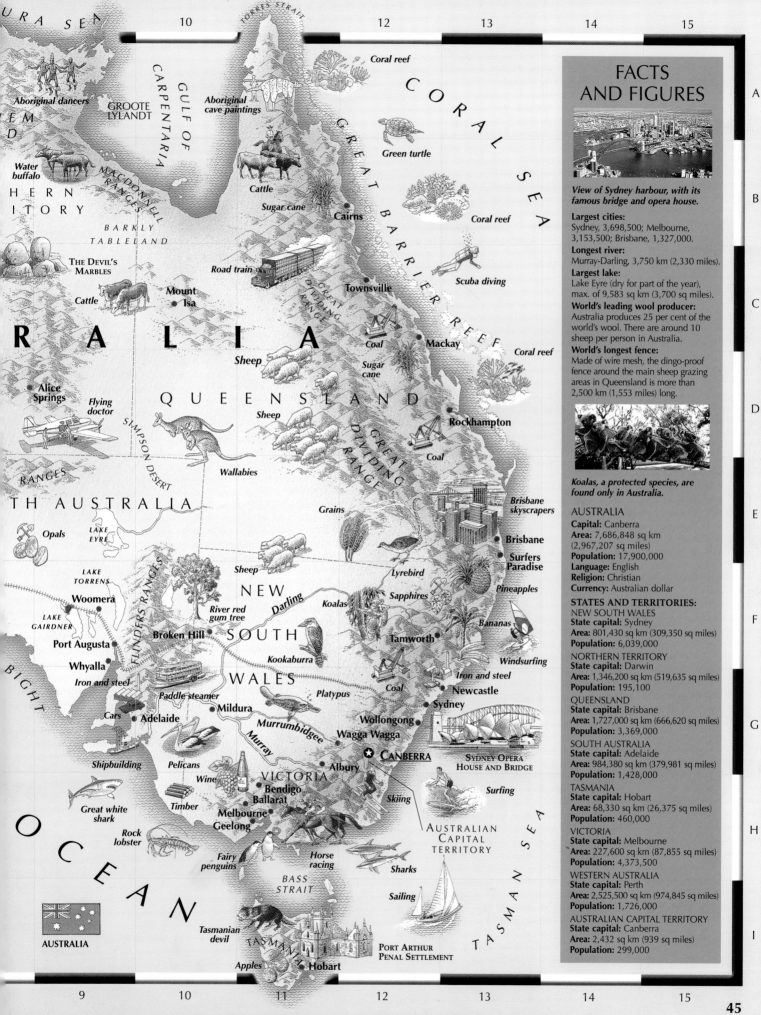

URA SEA

10 12 13 14 15

TORRES STRAIT

Coral reef

Aboriginal dancers

GROOTE
EYLANDT

GULF OF CARPENTARIA

Aboriginal cave paintings

CORAL SEA

Green turtle

Water buffalo

HERN
ITORY

MACDONNELL RANGES

BARKLY
TABLELAND

Cattle

Sugar cane

Cairns

GREAT BARRIER REEF

Coral reef

THE DEVIL'S MARBLES

Cattle

Mount Isa

Road train

GREAT DIVIDING RANGE

Townsville

Scuba diving

Coral reef

RALIA

Coal

Mackay

Coral reef

Alice Springs

Sheep

QUEENSLAND

Sugar cane

Flying doctor

SIMPSON DESERT

Sheep

GREAT DIVIDING RANGE

Rockhampton

RANGES

Wallabies

Coal

TH AUSTRALIA

Grains

Brisbane skyscrapers

Opals

LAKE EYRE

Brisbane

Surfers Paradise

LAKE TORRENS

Sheep

NEW

Lyrebird

Pineapples

Woomera

FLINDERS RANGES

River red gum tree

Darling

Koalas

Sapphires

LAKE GAIRDNER

Port Augusta

Broken Hill

SOUTH

Tamworth

Bananas

Whyalla

Iron and steel

Kookaburra

WALES

Coal

Iron and steel

Windsurfing

BIGHT

Paddle steamer

Cars

Adelaide

Mildura

Platypus

Newcastle

Sydney

Wollongong

Shipbuilding

Pelicans

Murrumbidgee

Murray

Wagga Wagga

CANBERRA

SYDNEY OPERA HOUSE AND BRIDGE

Great white shark

Wine

VICTORIA

Albury

Skiing

Surfing

Rock lobster

Timber

Bendigo
Ballarat

AUSTRALIAN CAPITAL TERRITORY

Melbourne
Geelong

OCEAN

Fairy penguins

Horse racing

Sharks

TASMAN SEA

Sailing

BASS STRAIT

AUSTRALIA

Tasmanian devil

TASMANIA

PORT ARTHUR PENAL SETTLEMENT

Apples

Hobart

9 10 11 12 13 14 15

FACTS AND FIGURES

View of Sydney harbour, with its famous bridge and opera house.

Largest cities:
Sydney, 3,698,500; Melbourne, 3,153,500; Brisbane, 1,327,000.
Longest river:
Murray-Darling, 3,750 km (2,330 miles).
Largest lake:
Lake Eyre (dry for part of the year), max. of 9,583 sq km (3,700 sq miles).
World's leading wool producer:
Australia produces 25 per cent of the world's wool. There are around 10 sheep per person in Australia.
World's longest fence:
Made of wire mesh, the dingo-proof fence around the main sheep grazing areas in Queensland is more than 2,500 km (1,553 miles) long.

Koalas, a protected species, are found only in Australia.

AUSTRALIA
Capital: Canberra
Area: 7,686,848 sq km (2,967,207 sq miles)
Population: 17,900,000
Language: English
Religion: Christian
Currency: Australian dollar

STATES AND TERRITORIES:
NEW SOUTH WALES
State capital: Sydney
Area: 801,430 sq km (309,350 sq miles)
Population: 6,039,000
NORTHERN TERRITORY
State capital: Darwin
Area: 1,346,200 sq km (519,635 sq miles)
Population: 195,100
QUEENSLAND
State capital: Brisbane
Area: 1,727,000 sq km (666,620 sq miles)
Population: 3,369,000
SOUTH AUSTRALIA
State capital: Adelaide
Area: 984,380 sq km (379,981 sq miles)
Population: 1,428,000
TASMANIA
State capital: Hobart
Area: 68,330 sq km (26,375 sq miles)
Population: 460,000
VICTORIA
State capital: Melbourne
Area: 227,600 sq km (87,855 sq miles)
Population: 4,373,500
WESTERN AUSTRALIA
State capital: Perth
Area: 2,525,500 sq km (974,845 sq miles)
Population: 1,726,000
AUSTRALIAN CAPITAL TERRITORY
State capital: Canberra
Area: 2,432 sq km (939 sq miles)
Population: 299,000

A
B
C
D
E
F
G
H
I

NEW ZEALAND

MADE UP OF two main islands – North Island and South Island – New Zealand lies about 1,600 km (1,000 miles) off Australia. Most people live on North Island, which has a tropical climate. The first settlers were the Maoris, who arrived from Polynesia around AD 900. The first European was the Dutch explorer Abel Tasman in 1642. New Zealand became a British colony in 1840 and gained independence in 1907. Today, the population is mainly a mix of Maoris and people of British descent.

MAP QUIZ

+ What is the alternative name for Mount Taranaki?

+ Which sea lies off the west coast of South Island?

+ Name the largest mountain range in New Zealand.

+ What makes the main Parliament Buildings in Wellington so unusual?

+ Which traditional Maori dance could you see performed on North Island?

Oysters

Tourism

Whangarei

Kauri pine

Snapper

Sailing

HAURAKI GULF

Iron and steel

Auckland

Windsurfing

BAY OF PLENTY

Dairy cattle

Maori carving

NORTH ISLAND

Hamilton

Tauranga

Kiwi fruit

Rotorua

Waikato

LAKE TAUPO

MT TARANAKI (MT EGMONT) 2,518 M

Oil and gas

New Plymouth

Gisborne

Haka (Maori dance)

HAWKE BAY

Snapper

Wanganui

Hastings

Napier

Palmerston North

Gannets

TASMAN BAY

COOK STRAIT

WELLINGTON

Nelson

Blenheim

PARLIAMENT BUILDINGS (WELLINGTON)

Apples

NEW ZEALAND

Kiwi

Sheep

Kaikoura

Greymouth

MT COOK 3,744 m

SOUTHERN ALPS

CHRISTCHURCH CATHEDRAL

Christchurch

NEW ZEALAND

Sperm whale

PACIFIC OCEAN

TASMAN SEA

SOUTH ISLAND

CANTERBURY PLAINS

Takahe

Textiles

Timaru

MILFORD SOUND

Skiing

Sheep

Tarakihi

Royal albatross

Kakapo

Apricots

Dunedin

Rugby

Invercargill

Rock lobster

FOVEAUX STRAIT

STEWART ISLAND

| 0 | 50 | 100 | 150 | 200 | 250 Kilometres |

| 0 | 50 | 100 | 150 Miles |

FACTS AND FIGURES

Auckland lies between Waitemata and Manukau Harbours.

NEW ZEALAND
Capital: Wellington
Area: 268,676 sq km (103,736 sq miles)
Population: 4,000,000
Languages: English, Maori
Religion: Christian
Currency: New Zealand dollar
Government: Parliamentary democracy

Largest lake:
Lake Taupo, 606 sq km (234 sq miles)
Longest river:
Waikato, 425 km (264 miles).
Largest cities:
Auckland, 966,300; Wellington, 404,200; Christchurch, 308,200.

Inlets shape the South Island coast.

INDEX

This index contains the most important place and feature names. The page number is given in **bold** type after the place name. The grid reference follows in lighter type.

M
Maastricht, Netherlands 13 G8
Macau, China 41 I11
Macedonia 23 F11
Mackay (City), Australia 45 C12
Madagascar 43 I11, 71 J19
Madeira (Island) 19 H11
Madeira (River), Brazil 30 D7
Madrid, Spain 19 D8
Majorca (Island) 19 I3
Malaga, Spain 18 H7
Malawi 43 G10
Malaysia 38 F5
Mali 42 B6
Mallorca (Island) 19 E13
Malmö, Sweden 14 I7
Malta (Island) 21 F15
Managua, Nicaragua 29 H8
Manaus, Brazil 30 E6
Manama, Bahrain 33 E10
Manchester, UK 9 F9
Manila, Philippines 39 C9
Man, Isle of 9 E8
Manitoba (Province), Canada 27 B9
Maputo, Mozambique 43 G12
Marseille, France 11 H11
Massif Central (Mts), France 11 F9
Mauritania 42 A6
Mecca, Saudi Arabia 32 G7
Medina, Saudi Arabia 32 F7
Mekong (River) 38 B4, 40 H8
Melbourne, Australia 45 H10
Messina, Sicily 21 G13
Mexico, North America 28 E3
Mexico City, Mexico 28 G5
Mexico, Gulf of, North America 26 I10, 28 F6
Miami, USA 27 I13
Michigan, Lake, USA 27 E11
Milan, Italy 20 C6
Minneapolis, USA 27 E9
Mississippi (River), USA 27 E10
Missouri (River), USA 27 F9
Mogadishu, Somalia 43 I8
Moldova 24 G1
Mombasa, Kenya 43 H9
Monaco 11 H12
Mongolia 40 B7
Monterrey, Mexico 28 E5
Montevideo, Uruguay 31 F12
Montreal, Canada 27 D12
Morocco 42 B4
Moscow, Rus. Fed. 24 C7
Mozambique 43 G12
Mumbai (Bombay), India 34 F6
Munich, Germany 16 G8
Murmansk, Rus. Fed. 25 A8
Murray (River), Australia 45 G11
Muscat, Oman 33 F12

N
Nagasaki, Japan 37 A13
Nairobi, Kenya 43 H9
Namib Desert, Namibia 43 E12
Namibia 43 E11
Naples, Italy 21 F10
Narvik, Norway 15 B9
Nashville, USA 27 G11
Nassua, Bahamas 29 D10
Negro (River), Brazil 30 D5
Nelson (River), Canada 27 B9
Nepal 35 D4
Netherlands 12 F5
Nevada (State), USA 26 F5
New Brunswick (Province), Canada 27 C14
Newcastle, Australia 45 G13
Newcastle Upon Tyne, UK 8 G8
New Delhi, India 34 D7
Newfoundland (Province), Canada 27 A14
Newfoundland (Island) 27 B15
New Guinea (Island) 39 G13
New Orleans, USA 27 H11
New South Wales (State),

Australia 45 F11
New York (City), USA 27 E13
New Zealand 46 F6
Niagara Falls, Canada-USA 27 E12
Nicaragua 29 H8
Nice, France 11 H12
Nicosia, Cyprus 32 C6
Niger 42 C7
Nigeria 42 C7
Nile (River), Egypt 42 C5
Northern Ireland, UK 8 D8
Northern Territory, Australia 44 B8
North Island, Pacific Ocean 46 C4
North Korea 41 D13
North Pole, Arctic Ocean 6 F4
Northwest Territories (Province), Canada 26 A7
Norway 14 F6
Nottingham, UK 9 G10
Nova Scotia (Province), Canada 27 D14
Nuremberg, Germany 16 F7
Nunavut (Province), Canada 26 A8
Nyasa, Lake, Malawi-Mozambique 43 G10

O
Ob' (River), Rus. Fed. 25 C9
Odesa, Ukraine 24 H2
Oklahoma City, USA 27 G9
Omaha, USA 27 F9
Oman 33 G11
Ontario, Lake, Canada-USA 22 E12
Ontario (Province), Canada 27 C10
Orinoco (River), Venezuela 30 D4
Orléans, France 11 D8
Osaka, Japan 37 E11
Oslo, Norway 14 G7
Ostend, Belgium 12 B7
Ottawa, Canada 27 D12
Oxford, UK 9 G11

P
Pakistan 34 C4
Palermo, Sicily 21 E13
Palma, Mallorca 19 E13
Pamplona, Spain 19 B10
Panama 29 I10
Panama City, Panama 29 I10
Papua New Guinea 39 G13
Paraguay 31 E9
Paraná (River), Argentina-Brazil 31 E10
Paris, France 11 C9
Pennines (Mts), UK 9 F8
Perth, Australia 44 F4
Peru 30 B6
Phnom Penh, Cambodia 38 D5
Phoenix, USA 26 G6
Phuket, Thailand 38 E3
Pisa, Italy 20 C7
Po (River), Italy 20 C6
Poland 22 G4
Port Augusta, Australia 45 F9
Port-au-Prince, Haiti 29 F12
Portland, USA 26 D5
Porto, Portugal 18 C4
Portugal 18 E4
Potsdam, Germany 17 C9
Poznan, Poland 22 G5
Prague, Czech Republic 22 H6
Pretoria, South Africa 43 G12
Puerto Rico (Island) 29 F13
Punta Arenas, Chile 31 C15
Purús (River), Brazil 30 D7
Pyrenees (Mts), France-Spain 10 I7, 18 B10

Q, R
Qatar 33 F10
Quebec (City), Canada 27 C13
Quebec (Province), Canada 27 C12
Queensland (State), Australia 45 D10
Quito, Colombia 30 A5

Rabat, Morocco 42 B4
Rangoon, Burma 35 F12
Recife, Brazil 30 I7
Reggio di Calabria, Italy 21 G13
Regina, Canada 26 C7
Reykjavik, Iceland 14 H2
Rhine (River) 12 G6, 16 D5
Rhode Island (State), USA 27 E13
Rhodes (Island), Greece 23 C14
Rhône (River), France 11 G10
Richmond, USA 27 F13
Riga, Latvia 24 D4
Rio de Janeiro, Brazil 31 H9
Rio Grande (River), Mexico-USA 26 I8, 28 D5
Riyadh, Saudi Arabia 33 F9
Rockhampton, Australia 45 D13
Rocky Mts, Canada-USA 26 B5
Romania 23 E8
Rome, Italy 21 E9
Rostock, Germany 17 B9
Rostov-na-Donu, Rus. Fed. 24 C6
Rotorua, New Zealand 46 D6
Rotterdam, Netherlands 12 E6
Russian Federation 6 E7, 25 C9
Rwanda 43 G9

S
Saarbrücken, Germany 16 F6
Sahara Desert, Africa 42 D5
St John's, Canada 27 B15
St Kitts & Nevis (Islands) 29 E14
St Lawrence (River), Canada 27 D13
St Louis, USA 27 F10
St Lucia (Island) 29 F15
St Petersburg, Rus. Fed. 24 B7
St Vincent and the Grenadines (Islands), 29 F15
Salado (River), Argentina 31 E10
Salamanca, Spain 18 D6
Salt Lake City, USA 26 E6
Salvador, Brazil 30 I8
Salween (River), Burma-China 40 G7
Salzburg, Austria 17 H9
Sana, Yemen 33 I8
San Antonio, USA 27 H9
San Diego, USA 26 G5
San Francisco, USA 26 F4
San José, Costa Rica 29 I9
San Juan, Puerto Rico 29 E13
San Salvador, El Salvador 28 H7
Santa Cruz, Tenerife 19 H13
Santander, Spain 18 A8
Santiago, Chile 31 C11
Santo Domingo, Dominican Republic 29 F12
São Francisco (River), Brazil 30 H8
Saône (River), France 11 E10
São Paulo, Brazil 31 G10
São Tomé and Príncipe (Islands) 43 C8
Sapporo, Japan 36 G3
Sarajevo, Bosnia and Herzegovina 23 G10
Sardinia (Island) 21 C11
Saskatchewan (Province), Canada 26 C7
Saudi Arabia 32 E7
Sava (River) 23 G9
Scilly, Isles of 9 D13
Scotland, UK 8 D6
Seattle, USA 26 C5
Segovia, Spain 18 D7
Seine (River), France 10 B7
Senegal 42 A6
Seoul, South Korea 41 D12
Severn (River), UK 9 F10
Seville, Spain 18 G7
Seychelles (Islands) 43 I10
Shannon (River), Ireland 9 B10
Sheffield, UK 9 G10
Shetland Islands 8 G2
Shikoku (Island) 37 C12

Shiraz, Iran 33 D11
Sicily (Island) 21 F14
Sierra Leone 42 A7
Singapore 38 F5
Skopje, Macedonia 23 F11
Slovakia 22 F7
Slovenia 23 H8
Sofia, Bulgaria 23 E10
Somalia 43 I8
South Africa 43 E13
Southampton, UK 9 G12
South Australia (State), Australia 44 E7
South Dakota (State), USA 26 E8
Southern Alps (Mts), New Zealand 46 H1
South Island 46 G1
South Korea 41 E13
South Pole, Antarctica 7 F4
Spain 18 C7
Sri Lanka 34 H9
Stanley, Falkland Islands 31 I11
Stavanger, Norway 14 G5
Stewart Island 46 H2
Stockholm, Sweden 15 G9
Strasbourg, France 11 C12
Stratford-upon-Avon, UK 9 G11
Stuttgart, Germany 16 G7
Sudan 42 F6
Sugar Loaf Mt, Brazil 31 H9
Sumatra (Island) 38 F4
Superior, Lake, Canada-USA 27 D10
Surinam 30 F4
Swansea, UK 9 E11
Swaziland 43 G12
Sweden 15 G8
Switzerland 16 H5
Sydney, Australia 45 G12
Syria 32 C7

T
Tabriz, Iran 33 B9
Tagus (River) Portugal-Spain 18 E4
T'aipei, Taiwan 41 H12
Taiwan 41 H12
Tajikistan 24 F8
Taklimakan (Desert), Asia 40 D5
Tampa, USA 27 I12
Tanganyika, Lake, Africa 43 G9
Tangier, Morocco 42 B4
Tanzania 43 G9
Tashkent, Uzbekistan 24 F7
Tasmania (State), Australia 45 I11
Taupo, Lake, New Zealand 46 D6
Tbilisi, Georgia 24 D6
Tehran, Iran 33 C10
Tel Aviv-Yafo, Israel 32 C6
Tennessee (State), USA 27 G11
Texas (State), USA 27 H8
Thailand 38 C4
Thames (River), UK 9 H12
Thessaloniki, Greece 23 D12
Tiber (River), Italy 21 E9
Tibet (Xizang) 40 E5
Tigris (River), Iraq 33 C9
Tijuana, Mexico 28 C1
Timor (Island) 39 I9
Tirana, Albania 23 G11
Titicaca, Lake, Bolivia-Peru 31 C8
Togo 42 C7
Tokyo, Japan 37 H9
Toledo, Spain 18 E8
Toronto, Canada 27 E12
Toulouse, France 11 H8
Tournai, Belgium 13 C9
Toyama, Japan 37 F9
Trent (River), UK 9 G10
Trieste, Italy 20 F6
Trinidad and Tobago (Islands) 29 G15
Tripoli, Libya 42 E4
Tromsø, Norway 15 A10
Trondheim, Norway 14 D7
Trujillo, Peru 30 A7

Tunis, Tunisia 42 D3
Tunisia 42 D4
Turin, Italy 20 B6
Turkey 32 A6
Turkmenistan 24 E7

U, V
Uganda 43 G8
Ukraine 24 G2
United Arab Emirates 33 F11
United States of America 26 H2
Uruguay (Country) 31 E11
Uruguay (River), Uruguay 31 E11
Ural Mts, Rus. Fed. 25 C8
Ürümqi, China 40 C6
Utrecht, Netherlands 12 F5
Uzbekistan 24 E7
Valencia, Spain 19 E10
Valladolid, Spain 18 C7
Valletta, Malta 21 F15
Valparaíso, Chile 31 C11
Van, Lake, Turkey 33 B8
Vancouver (City), Canada 26 C5
Vatican City 21 E9
Venezuela 30 C4
Venice, Italy 20 E6
Veracruz, Mexico 28 C6
Vermont (State), USA 27 D13
Verona, Italy 20 D6
Victoria, Lake, Africa 43 G9
Victoria (State), Australia 45 H11
Victoria Falls, Zambia-Zimbabwe 43 F11
Vienna, Austria 17 G11
Vientiane, Laos 38 B5
Vietnam 38 B4
Vigo, Spain 18 B4
Vilnius, Lithuania 24 E3
Vladivostock, Rus. Fed. 25 E14
Volga (River), Rus. Fed. 24 C7
Volgograd, Rus. Fed. 24 D7

W, X, Y, Z
Wales, UK 9 E11
Wanganui, New Zealand 46 E5
Warsaw, Poland 22 F5
Washington DC, USA 27 F12
Waterford, Ireland 9 C11
Wellington, New Zealand 46 E5
Western Australia (State), Australia 44 D5
Western Sahara, Africa 42 A5
West Virginia (State), USA 27 F12
Whangarei, New Zealand 46 B5
Wight, Isle of 9 G13
Windhoek, Namibia 43 E12
Winnipeg, Canada 27 C9
Winnipeg, Lake, Canada 27 C9
Wroclaw, Poland 22 G5
Wuhan, China 41 F11
Wuwei, China 41 E8
Xi'an, China 41 F10
Xingu (River), Brazil 30 F6
Yamoussouke, Ivory Coast 42 B8
Yangtze (River), China 40 G8
Yekaterinburg, Rus. Fed. 25 D8
Yellow River, China 41 E11
Yemen 33 H9
Yenisey (River), Rus. Fed. 25 C10
Yerevan, Armenia 24 D6
Yokohama, Japan 37 G9
Yugoslavia 23 F10
Zagreb, Croatia 23 H8
Zagros Mts, Iran 33 E11
Zambezi (River), Mozambique-Zambia 43 F11
Zaragoza, Spain 19 C10
Zhengzhou, China 41 F10
Zimbabwe 43 G11
Zurich, Switzerland 16 H6

Abbreviation:
Rus. Fed. = Russian Federation